STICKS & STONES & GRAVY BONES

squirrels, cats and life through my eyes

by
Shaggy Johnson Lane,
Bichon *extraordinero*

Discript

First published in the United Kingdom by
Discript Limited
67 Fishbourne Road West
Chichester
West Sussex
PO19 3JJ

www.discript.com

A catalogue record for this book is available from the British Library

ISBN 978–1–9163613–1–7

Designed and typeset in Warnock Pro by Discript Ltd
Printed in Scotland by Bell & Bain Ltd

Dedicated to Greybeard
(aka Richard Johnson)
for his encouragement and support for every project
that I have undertaken over the years.

Acknowledgements

Thanks to the wonderful Barbara Horn Jacobson for editing paw prints and all.

Dramatis Caninos

Shaggy	deep thinker and author, a Bichon
Chiquita	Shaggy's cuddly twin sister
Jimmy	French minature longhaired Dachshund
Lola	movie-star Fox Terrier
Bertie	nice Norfolk (or is it Norwich?) Terrier
Harry	wise old King Charles Spaniel
Pippa	sister of Harry and full of fun
Marnie	Irish Jackiepoo
Toby	elderly Japanese Yorkie
Manchas	agile tree climber, Jack Russell
Beyoncé (Bea)	pocket-sized Dachshund
Billy	Norfolk Terrier, known as Billy No Mates
Oscar	wee sweet Shih Tzu
Lily	elegant Lurcher
Flo	pocket-sized wirehaired Dachshund
Clemmie	sister of Flo
Ruby	Pit Bull Terrier with the biggest smile
Indigo	americano Schnauzer
Luna	window-gazing Beagle
Roddy	good-natured Labrador
Ernie	large wirehaired Dachshund

Tristan	Shih Tzu who is sensitive about how his breed name is pronounced.
Pumpkin	puddle-loving Shih Tzu
Rasmus	Danish Bichon
Alfie	Bichon, bestest friend and neighbour from Shaggy's youth
Chai Latte	Maltese Terrier, bestest friend from Shaggy's past life
Toby	Chinese Bichon
Oliver	brother of Toby
Herbie	cuddly Norfolk Terrier
Smudge	Cavachon
Neddy	Jack Russell
Caspar	yodelling Schnauzer

NOW IN RAINBOW BRIDGE

Candy	diva Cocker Spaniel
Maggie	miniature Dachshund who went blind and slightly doolally after being left in a very hot car
Scamp	lovable King Charles Spaniel
Alfie	Norfolk Terrier who loved reiki sessions
Henry	Maltese Terrier who could pee walking on his front paws
Carlo	football playing Bassett Hound
Hugo	little Chihuahua (or 'wa-wa'), kennel mate of Carlo
Senf	smooth-haired Dachshund

Hello, everyone!

With the best of good intentions, I started out by sending my manuscript to a publisher and was really pawstricken when they sent me a rude letter. My literary efforts were brutally rejected. No ifs, no buts, just this:

Dear Contributor,

We are returning your stupid story. You are a terrible writer: Why did you bother sending it to us? We wouldn't buy your story even if you paid us.

Don't contact us again

Drop dead.

Get lost.

Take your gravy bones elsewhere.

The Man with the Beard (Greybeard) told me not to take it personally, as it was probably a standard rejection slip. He said, "I'll get it published for you. Just go ahead and type out your life story."

Before we begin

I am having such an exciting life and, with so much persuasion from all my doggy friends, just thought I would keep a log of how my new life is going right now.

It certainly has been a whirlwind of sniffing endless bottoms and rolling in many stinky things. So far it has been hectic, interesting and exciting.

Aside from staring out of the window at the garden, having the occasional scratch and licking my balls, my entire day is focused on walkies and dinner.

Will it be pellets or something tasty from a tin or even human left-overs? I enjoy all of these with a bowl of Pawsecco. Yummy! My! How my life has changed in the last 18 months.

How it all began

My past life is a bit vague.

My twin sister, Chiquita, and I, aka Schlagarone, are Bichons born in Costa Rica. It may have been somewhere else quite mundane, like a puppy farm, but it sounds really glamorous to tell everyone that our place of birth was Costa Rica. Our original owner – Mum – was from Costa Rica. We lived with her in a flat in Maida Vale, London and travelled with her to many places in Europe. We know that, because people open my passport and show me the stamps and tell me that my sister and I are well-travelled puppies. Mum is now in a nursing home. We loved her a lot, but when she became ill, we moved in with Auntie Viv.

Auntie lived in a pretty house with a pretty garden and a pretty little white Maltese terrier named Chai Latte. We went for walks, we ate well and we played with Chai all day. Our nextdoor neighbour was Alfie, another Bichon, and he was good fun too. He joined in with our zoomies – a zoomie is a doggy mad moment of happiness spent dashing flat out usually in a circle – and playtime. Yes! Life couldn't have been nicer. But all good things have to come to an end.

We had been with Auntie for several months when one day she sat us down and said, sadly, "I'm afraid I can't keep you both and will have to consider finding you a new home and a new owner." Chiquita was upset and became teary and said, "What if we are separated and put with different people. I will never get to see you again. How will I cope, Shaggy?" There was a grave danger that we might be put down if a suitable home couldn't be found for us. I don't even know what that means. Down on the floor... down in our baskets... down where?

A few days later Auntie said, "C'mon, we're going visiting. I'm taking you to meet some lovely people who love dogs and who you might like." She took us to the house of Greybeard and the Woman. I really liked them. They were so kind and gentle. They had a big garden and a houseful of interesting smells and, best of all, a box of stinky, smelly well chewed-up toys. Exactly how I like them. We had a wonderful day of exploring, running in and out of the garden, and yapping at birds and squirrels.

Settling in

Auntie stayed for lunch and chatted while we happily checked the house and garden out. Chiquita said, "This is nice here, innit!" After lunch Auntie handed over our luggage and said, "Now you be good and I will see you both soon." We settled in with these new people and life became busy and exciting. However, on the first day we thought that they could turn out to be Bichon killers. I must admit I was pretty stupid that first day. I cringed by the front door for half an hour after Auntie left us, but the Woman said, "C'mon! let's not be stupid about this. You are with us for the rest of your lives, so make the best of it." Then she gave me a treat and a little cuddle and I thought, "Hmmm, these people are not too bad. They haven't killed me or Chiquita yet." Chiquita, by the way, is a very chilled out little creature and always makes the best of any situation. When I got tearful and missed Auntie and Chai Latte, she said "You've always got me, Schlags." We chatter away in Spanish and that's good. The Woman has learned a few words and is always yelling *Aquí* for "come here", and *Callate* for "shut up". My English is getting better and I now know the important words, like "treats", "walkies", "shut up", "don't" ... and "come here".

We have many lovely beds in every room in the house to crash out on. My favourite is a big bed that, I understand, belonged to a basset hound named Carlo. The best bed of all is the huge king-size bed that belongs to Greybeard and the Woman. We all snuggle up together at night and it is doggy heaven.

The Woman was telling us about Carlo and his Chihuahua brother named Hugo. They lived with Greybeard and Woman for five years. According to the Woman, Carlo was a character and well known in the park for his football skills. He was the doggy equivalent of Ronaldo and played a mean game. He would join a game with humans and leave them open mouthed with his dribbling skills. The Woman told me that he was a beautiful specimen of a dog – lean and sleek like a bullet. He was a softie who would creep onto the human's bed and take up the entire bed so that Greybeard would be hanging onto the sides. Every night he was kicked off and made to sleep in his own bed, but he would creep back. His little brother, Hugo, was the Woman's favourite and would always cuddle up with her on the settee. She was very tearful when they went back to their owner. She said, "I knew Hugo was upset because his big eyes filled up with tears when he was put onto the plane. He said, 'I will never see you again, will I?' Carlo just told his little brother, 'Hey, man, chill! There is adventure waiting for us in Dubai. All that sun and sand to roll around in.'"

A boy by any other name

God alone knows why I was named Schlagarone, but the Woman said to Greybeard, "That's going to be changed. There is no way I am going to be screeching that name in the park. We are renaming him. How about Shaggy? It sounds similar." So Shaggy I became. I don't mind, It sounds good to me and Chiquita agrees that it's not a bad sounding name for a handsome white dog.

Three months after moving to our new home Chiquita and I had to go to Puppy University to take our silent farting exams. There was a room with a fierce looking judge sitting at a table and he asked us to give an example of the silent but deadly fart. He said, "Go ahead," so I did a "pfft" but the adjudicator said, "Sorry, young man, but you'll have to come back in six months for the next exam." So I'm afraid I failed this time, but it was nice to know that Chiquita passed with flying colours. She has excellent SBD (silent but deadly) skills.

She says it's because she is a girl and not so obvious as a man. Greybeard says, "I don't know why you bothered to take that exam, because you are pretty deadly with your silent farts and I can't understand why you failed the exam. The ones that you let off in the car after your walks are certainly pretty toxic." I get embarrassed and always apologise by giving him a kiss on his arm. He seems very good-natured about it. He always says, "Don't worry, Shags, all men do it."

Every day my sister and I get taken for lovely long walks in the park. The best bit is being off the lead. Auntie always kept us on the lead. The freedom is scary but also very enjoyable. We chase squirrels and birds, and it feels really good to be free. It has been a crazy, exciting few months for us.

I am a young lad with everything to live for. I have grabbed every opportunity to embrace my new life, and I have grabbed it with all four paws. Greybeard and Woman often ask, "Who's a good boy?" What if I never find out who is a good boy? I wag my tail and that makes them very happy.

A snarling handbagging in the park

The other day I had a hand-bagging barney in the park with a dreadfully rough and mangy mutt who called my sister a "snooty foreign bitch with more money than brains". That really made me angry, so I took a chunk out of his fur. The Woman separated us by getting hold of my tail and lifting me off the ground. The mutt screamed as though he was being killed and his owner screamed even louder. It was tremendously exciting. Woman said that I shouldn't do that too often, as she will would have to keep me on a lead and away from all the other dogs. She says neurotic owners spread the word that you are a vicious dog and that will give you a bad name and reputation. She said, "You don't want to be known as a delinquent dog."

There are two other Bichon Frises – our proper breed names – in the park who look identical to us and people are always blaming us for their behaviour. Not that they are bad, but you know how quick people are to attribute blame. Chiquita is in love with one of them and every time we see them, she rushes up to him, wiggles her bum and flirts outrageously. He turns his face away and says, "OKAY! Okay! Enough already. Let's not overdo the excitement at seeing me." He is quite sophisticated and doesn't like his girls to be so over the top.

I don't really know what my new owners do for a living but we are never short of treats. Woman laughs and says, "I have reinvented myself many times. I was a PR in international hotels, then I became a stylist for cookery books in the days when there were only 10 people in London doing it. Then I trained to be a make-up artist in film and television, and when the age of digital came in, I became a dog sitter and invited dogs to stay in our home." She also does dog reiki and homeopathy, so you can see she does many things and seems very talented at whatever she does. I love it when she gives me and my sister a massage.

Greybeard told me that he was a publisher and book designer. "See all those books on the shelf, Shaggy? I designed the covers." I think he now busies himself with ranting and waggling his finger when he is displeased, naming trees, weather forecasting, clouds, trying to freeze snowballs, Lego, group tiddlywinks and burping loudly. He has also become the daily laundry man, chief cook and bottle washer. He is always collapsing on the sofa, holding his forehead and saying "Oy vey! If you only knew the day I've had." Occasionally, he shouts if we bark too much.

Ninja costumes

It's raining really hard today but we still went to the park for a walk. I was given a dreadful red mackintosh to keep me dry. I hated it. I looked like the caped crusader. I wonder why the Woman dresses us up. She says, "There is nothing worse than getting into a car with the strong smell of wet mouldy fur." I often tell her, "Listen, lady, you are sadly mistaken if you think putting on these ridiculous outfits will convince us to go out in the rain to pee." In fact, I quite fancy a green cape like a Ninja turtle. Then I could hurtle around the park barking "Cow-a-bunga!" I saw that on television one day when I was lounging with my paws under my chin wondering about the meaning of an adopted dog's life and future.

Woman boards other dogs when their owners go on holidays. One of our group is a real pain. He is a black Pug named Basil and a real moaner. "Oh, god, not kibble again," he always says, and then he wolfs it down and gets indigestion. When we get to the park, he moans that it's a different place every day. He says, "I'm a creature of habit and don't like change. I'm too old in my ways to have constant stimulus." If he was human, he would be a professor of something because he is so serious and intense. A simple conversation between us dogs becomes a serious lecture on the quality of life as a dog.

We have a manic Jack Russell named Manchas spending the weekend with us. He is also a Spanish speaker and that's good. It stops us feeling homesick. Manchas is a pretty hyper character and his only dream in life is to catch a squirrel. We asked him what he would do with it if he did catch it, and he said, "Dunno, but I do enjoy the chase and climbing trees." Each day he does the same thing and we all roll our eyes at each other and say, "Tch! He's off again." The tourists love it. They stand around taking pictures on their camera phones and asking the Woman if a ladder is needed to get him down. He provides plenty of entertainment for them. I don't mind him climbing trees every day, ripping off the bark and barking like a mad thing, but when we are all settled in for the night, he starts grunting, yipping and twitching, and that makes the rest of us wake up and get nervous in case he dies. I wish he wouldn't do it. It's very unsettling.

I am now going to snuggle up to Greybeard and watch a bit of moving pictures on the black box that has voices coming out of it. Greybeard likes Scandi dramas and rugby. That's a game where many men chase a funny shaped ball. They sometimes look as though they are kicking each other just for pleasure and Greybeard says, "It's pretty rough, Shags. You would hate it – you would end up being kicked around like the ball because you are a small individual."

The Woman prefers to read newspapers and magazines and doesn't shout abuse at the big shiny box like Greybeard does. He is always shouting, "I CANNOT BELIEVE THIS!" at the box.

A new friend

A new member has joined the group for a few days. He is a Podenco named Panxo. It sounds posh but in reality I think it's Spanish for mutt. He is a Jack Russell cross who was born in Majorca. He had us all entranced with the stories of his life. He said he was born on a farm somewhere in the countryside and had many brothers and sisters. One day when he was a puppy, he decided to walk down the lane and do a bit of exploring. He ended up on the Via Cintura – a very busy motorway – and he said that it was very scary. I've never been there but I can imagine it must have been terrifying. Cars and big trucks thundering in both directions. When it got dark, he got lost, became starving hungry and just kept running for days. Then, one morning, a kind and caring Japanese couple coaxed him out from under bushes, carried him to every house and farm they came to and asked if he belonged there. After a week, they took him to a vet, had him chipped, gave him a bath to get rid of the fleas and then brought him to England.

He said he had never been so scared in his life: "I wanted my mum, brothers and sisters." He was put into a cage, loaded into a very loud, droning machine, and flown to England. When he arrived, he said, it was freezing cold and he was let out onto a strange type of floor. It was wet and green and he had never felt anything like it under his paws. I think he was very brave. He is quite clever, too, as he also speaks three languages. Chiquita loves his cute barking in Japanese. Chiquita thinks that she might be in love with him. I told her she could do worse, as he comes from a very wealthy family.

Panxo says he now has the most wonderful life. His owner is a millionaire and they live in a mansion with the biggest garden ever. They spends six months in England and six months in a beautiful house in Majorca. They also have a 62-foot yacht called Kir Royale. That puzzled Panxo, as Japanese people can't properly pronounce the initial R. He said it was wonderful to cruise the Med. He has his own motorised dinghy and a life jacket that he has to wear. He also has his own minder, who would take him to the nearest bit of land for a pee. "I loved going fast with the wind blowing in my ears. Faster! faster! I would be barking as we zoomed along." Panxo told us that his diet now consists of raw fish, rice balls and many other strange-tasting foods. He said that he often gets a longing for good old dog food and rubbish bin leftovers. I will say this for him: he is a great forager and finds some incredible things for us to munch in the park. This behaviour drives every owner mad because they say, "It could be something that will make you very sick. It costs money to have you treated by a vet."

Panxo says he has almost forgotten his Spanish, as his new owners speak to him in Japanese. Although he is not fluent, he does know the important words for "food", "walkies", "bath", "willy" and "you stink". We all sit around and jabber away in Spanish, as my mum and auntie were Costa Rican and that's what they spoke most. All the others tell us to speak in Doglish, saying it's unfair that they don't know what we are saying. They think we might be talking about them. Manchas often butts in, as he too comes from a Spanish home. He is always saying "Speak to the paw" when he doesn't want to hear something.

Tree climbing mates

This morning's walk was very interesting. We went to a different part of the park and met so many new dogs that all our heads are spinning. Manchas, of course, spent 25 minutes climbing as many trees as he could and the tourists stopped and stared. "Oh! Look!" they'd say, "There's a dog climbing trees. Do you think he needs help getting down?" I always tell the others: "Tell them that the dog will fall on their head, then when they are flat on their backs, they won't be so keen to help it get down."

The park was wet and sloshy and my paws felt really dirty. I found the most exquisite smell and showed the others where it was. It was Eau de Foxpoo. I was just about to throw myself on it when the Woman said: "Oh! No, you don't, any of you, and it's a shower for you, Shags, when we get home." Sure enough, when we got home, she dragged me into the shower room and blasted me with the power shower. The others peeked in and said that I looked like one of those cartoon characters splayed up against the wall. Chiquita, or Miss Tippy Toes, as we call her, said to me, "You never learn, do you? You know that every time you roll in something, she turns the shower on you. Humans don't appreciate the same sorts of smells as we do."

The reason for bottom sniffing

One of the things that I find most bewildering are the number of dogs who stick their noses in my bum. I've had a sheltered life and I find this behaviour gross. The Woman said, "Thank god, we humans don't greet each other by doing that." I asked Basil the Wise One why dogs do it and he said, pompously, "Legend has it that there was once a dog's party. All the dogs hung their bums on a coat rack before partying. Then someone shouted 'Fire' and there was a mad rush to the coat rack and they all picked the first bum they could get their paws on." Baz said, "That's the reason all the dogs sniff each other's bums, to see if it is their bum." You think that's a bit farfetched! Listen! I'm a dog. I will believe anything that you tell me!

The daily menu

Marnie, the very chilled out Jackapoo, stalked a stupid squirrel this morning. The squirrel was on the ground, all fat and fluffy, happily munching on a peanut donated by a tourist. It was totally unaware of Marnie stalking it and had no idea how close she was. We all stood very still and watched, then Marnie pounced and almost got the squirrel. We all barked and cheered afterwards and joined Marnie in chasing it until it leapt into another tree. We couldn't stop talking about it in the car on the way home. It was soooooooo exciting. I bet it will be a long time before that squirrel ventures onto the ground again and says to a tourist: "Please, sir, do you have a spare peanut?"

Came home to dinner – pellets and Pooched Salmon. Delicious! I don't mind staying here as long as the food remains as good as it was tonight. Every meal is different because the Woman says, "Dogs get bored with the same old kibble." Basil said, "I'll second that!" but then he moans that he doesn't like change.

Things that go whizz bang and light up the sky

The weekend was scary. The Woman told us that it was Guy Fawkes night and that many idiots would be letting off fireworks. I was okay with the noise of bangs and whistles but one or two of the gang hid under the chairs and refused to come out. Jimmy, the longhaired Dachshund, a very moody little dog, said that if you tremble hard enough, you get lots of cuddles, get fussed over and lots of treats. I wonder why some of the boy dogs don't pee on the boxes of fireworks. That will make them fizzle out. We all asked why anyone would spend so much money on things that burn in a few seconds. Think of all the tasty schmakoos you could buy with the price of a rocket. We were all allowed to huddle together on the bed with Greybeard and the Woman.

I could quite get used to it. Every time there was a big bang, we all jumped, then it all went quiet. The Woman got very angry and said that "people who waste money on fireworks should have their balls chopped off for scaring birds, animals and elderly people".

The cone of shame

"Do you know something?" I told the others, "I once had balls, but I was tricked by the Woman. One day she said, "C'mon, Shags, walkies in the park." And the next thing I knew was when I woke up on a table with many people checking and talking to me and when I looked down to check why I was hurting, I had no balls. I must admit, I did panic and make a lot of noise until a nice nurse calmed me down. The other dogs said, "It must have hurt", and I said, "Yes, it hurt like hell." I couldn't even lick myself, as they put a lampshade around my neck for a week. To add insult to injury, Greybeard played a trick on me by putting two balls on the ends of knitting needles so that they looked like olives and stuck them into the lampshade. He said I looked like a giant Martini; I think that's a human treat of some sort. The other thing I hated was that I was bouncing off the walls and the furniture and getting stuck in gaps because that damned collar was so big. The gang thought it was all very funny. I can tell you that I wasn't pleased about being the butt of everyone's jokes. Still, it did keep them amused.

After my operation to have my balls off, I find it disgusting that when we go to the park, all the male dogs want to have jiggy-jig with me by clamping themselves onto my back. Everyone, humans and dogs, keep yelling at me to bite them, then they will stop. Someone told me that it was a sign of dominance. I don't know if it's a good or a bad thing but when I had my balls, I would piddle anywhere and also hump any male that came within one foot of me. I was a right old jiggy bunny and up for a bit of humping anything. All the other boys told me that they were the same until they had their balls removed. The smell of testosterone must still linger, because all the males are keen on getting it on with me. I should try to butch up and then maybe they will leave me alone. Hopefully, it will pass and I will become just one of the boys.

Multi lingual mates

Manchas went home today and it was such a relief to all of us. He was so manic. He did everything at 300 miles an hour. All is peaceful in the house now. Chiquita hated him because, she said, "He is so uncouth and loud and muscles in on everything. He tries to hijack everyone's food." I don't know why he does that, because he lives in a big house with servants and he is waited on on all four paws. It's not as if he is starved at home.

We had a wonderful game of tag in the park with Jimmy. He speaks Greek, English and French, so I am learning lots of new words. I hope they aren't rude ones. I think tomorrow's walk will be a peaceful one now that Manchas has gone home.

I am beginning to love being here, although I still miss my Mum. I am beginning to forget her smell, but the Woman gives the nicest hugs I have ever had.

Just enjoyed a wonderful dinner of Beef Waggington and green beans plus a few of my pellets. I licked my plate clean. Ouf! that was really yummy.

Waddidya say?

 "What did you say?"
"I wasn't talking to you, I was talking to the dogs."

This is a daily conversation in this house. I never understand what Greybeard or the Woman says, but it sounds really nice and friendly every time they chat to us. "Would you like a treat?" It sounds like "mnn!mnn!mnn!" to us, although I now know the word "treat" because of the way that they put an emphasis on it! You learn when the words are good or angry, because with good words, they stroke you, and with bad words, they look cross and waggle their finger at you.

I like it when people tell me that I look like one of those 1920s movie dogs. There's one particular creaky old Labrador, named Barney, who says to Chiquita every morning, "By god, you're a fine-looking filly! If I were 20 years younger I would go for you in a big way." His owner says, "Don't mind him. He's an old letch! He is just too old to get his leg over anything." So that's all right, then! Poor old boy! He has terrible difficulty in moving around because his bones are stiff. I asked him if he is taking any medication and he told me, "I am stuffed with pills, potions and magic bones, but when you get old, you get old, laddie."

Marnie went home this morning. We will all miss her because she is so chilled and calm. She could be very amusing as well, and she kept us all happy by talking about many things. I was very surprised at how excited she got when she saw her mum. She screamed and screamed and yipped so loudly that I am sure she could be heard at the end of the street. We all went outside with her to say goodbye. We promised we would keep in touch, but we never do, do we? Once we get home, we forget everything.

At the same time that Marnie left, two new dogs arrived to stay for two weeks. Harry, the King Charles Spaniel, and his baby sister, Pippa, who is as slim as an eel. He is a bit of a know-it-all and immediately started a discussion with me about his biggest concern, which is global warming, climate change, melting ice caps, and other terrifying things happening to the world. I could feel my eyes rolling back in my head. Then he said to Chiquita, "And you! young lady, what worries you most in this day and age?" She said the first thing that came into her head: "Food! I worry that I will never get any." He said, "Tch, tch! That's the trouble with youth today. You really should take things more seriously."

Pippa bounced in and said, "Don't pay attention to him, he talks utter garbage but would kill for a bowl of kibble at any time of the day." We are going to get on well, as she is bouncy, pretty and doesn't take life so seriously. I feel that whenever Harry comes to stay, he will bore us rigid with his views on politics, global warming, food allergies, the correct way to poo, the rights of canines in the parks and whether Rainbow Bridge actually exists. Woman says that Harryoake (as she calls him) is the senior dog in the pack and that what he tells us to do goes because she has given him permission to boss us around. And to think that I've got two weeks of him to put up with. Sheesh!

Every meeting is a social event

Wow, what a great walk we had this morning! We met so many new dogs. My head is buzzing with all the gossip that we caught up on, plus reading all the new pee mails. The gang were shouting out to each other, "Come over here. Here's a great pee mail left by a Pitbull named Ruby. Isn't it witty?" "Here's one left by that aggressive cockerpoo. You have to feel sorry for him because he only gets one walk a day and then he is left indoors for many hours while his parents go out to work. He said he has given up shredding cushions and other things, as he gets traumatised by the yelling they do. It's a boring life. Here's one from that ageing bitch who lives in that mansion in Primrose Hill." And here's a terrific one from Caspar, the yodelling schnauzer who tells us that he dreams of becoming the winner of *Britain's Got Talent* and getting famous for being the UK's first canine yodeller.

We met our dear old friend Alfie, our nextdoor neighbour when we stayed with Auntie. Chiquita was so pleased to see Alfie that she did a delighted zoomie for three minutes. It was such an infectious gesture and it looked like so much fun that we all joined in. Then some more dogs joined in to the delight of the dog owners. When we all stopped, we said to each other, "Ouf! wasn't that fun? We will do it again soon, eh!"

Gosh, we've had an eventful afternoon. The Woman was gardening and we were all sniffing around, rolling on earthworms, digging up the flowerbeds and finding new things to eat, when Jimmy disappeared through the fencing. Pippa and I saw him in another garden and started barking at him. He got cross said that they were "snitches" and that they had spoiled his fun. The Woman was really, really cross, because he wouldn't come back and it took 25 minutes to get him near enough to the fencing to grab his collar and drag him through. He is a strange little soul. He never really interacts with anyone in the group. I am sure he is going to suffer doggy dementia when he gets older, because he sometimes just sits and stares into nothingness, then if you poke your nose into his bum, he jumps into life and scoots off. He is going home tonight. Will we notice that he has gone? I don't think so. On the other hand, he could be quite good fun when he was in the right mood.

Dinner tonight is going to be Bowl-licking Chicken and mushy peas with kibble.

Leaves are for scuffing in

I love these winter walks. Piles of leaves fallen everywhere and its good fun racing through them before we all do our poos. The poor Woman is rushing everywhere trying to pick up and has to hunt like mad for it in the fallen leaves.

We were all asking each other, "Why do they pick up our poo? We don't do it to them when they use the loo. It's probably a human thing. What do they do with it?" Wise Harry told us that some people put it in their handbag and dispose of it at home. He said, "I heard of a lady who had her handbag snatched. Imagine the thieves' reaction when they put their hands inside the bag to discover the contents."

Another thing that puzzled us is that you never see Greybeard and the Woman peeing or pooing in public. I told everyone, "It's because they have only got two legs, so if they lifted one to do a pee, they would probably topple over and hurt themselves."

Our evening walks are very exciting. We rush around in the dark, staying together. After all, you never know if the bogeyman will get you. Luckily, the Woman has fitted us all with little flashing lights on our collars. Jimmy said, "Mon dieu, I hate looking like a glowworm with this thing on my collar." Pippa, who has a sense of humour, retorted, "Live with it, Saucisson, because you ain't seen nothing yet. Wait until Christmas, when you get the full Christmas outfit, with flashing lights and antler horns. Then you can hide in the bushes in shame after they have photographed you from every angle, and posted pictures on social media. It's so embarrassing!"

The good thing is that the Woman wears a flashing light, too, so that we all know where she is.

A disastrous but memorable walk

Today's walk was a disaster. We were all busy sniffing around when Pippa, who is as thin as an eel, said to us "I've always wanted to see what it's like in that big house", so she squeezed though the railings and was off exploring. The Woman got very agitated and called Pip's name for an hour. We could all hear her yapping with excitement. Then a kind park keeper went to the gate of the Big House and told the security guard that a dog had got into their property. The Woman kept saying, "I'm going to kill that sodding dog when I get her." We all decided it would be better to stick together and be obedient because the Woman was spitting mad. She took us back to the car and we waited quietly. Greybeard said, "Never mind gang, we'll give you a nice long walk this evening." Pips was chased everywhere and she thought it was a wonderful game. She said it was an amazing garden with nooks and caves full of hiding places. She really gave them a merry dance. Two security guards, three gardeners and the Woman finally caught Pippa. When she got back to the car, the Woman said, "Dont even talk to me, Pip. You lose all your privileges. From now on you stay joined to Harry. Tough luck, Harry!" "Harry rolled his eyes and moaned, "That's my walks ruined for the next two weeks. I can't wait for you to grow up and become a responsible adult." Pippa just grinned, kissed him and said, "Yeah, yeah Chill, why don't you?" The security guard thought that Pippa was lovely, but the gardeners thought that she was a wicked little fleabag. The Woman said, "That's nothing to what I think of her."

Wawas

Eric, the little "Wawa" – Chihuahua to you – from next door has come to stay for three nights. I often hear him shouting out "Yoo hoo!" to us from his garden when we go out to ours. Very handsome and rather sweet like a cuddly toy, when he comes to our house, he spends all day buried under the bedcovers or hiding underneath a chair that has a frill. Anytime any one goes near the chair, he attacks like a piranha fish, snarling and snapping. I asked him, "What is your problem? Are you a social misfit? Try being nice to us and we will be nice to you." "Oh! Okay," he said and has since been as nice as pie. He even let me smell his bottom and when we were sitting together, he put his paw around my shoulder. That made Greybeard and the Woman coo with pleasure. They got out their phones and took many pictures of him with his arm around me. He was raised as a puppy by a pretty housecat named Bailey. He told us that he considers Bailey his mum. He uses a litter tray and when he is licking his balls, he sits exactly like the cat. He is getting better at socialising and he says that we make him feel really welcome when he comes to stay. We like him a lot. But, then, I must say, we always make everyone feel welcome. There's no point in being nasty, is there? I am always proud of the fact that Chiquita and I are just nice caninos.

I am really enjoying living at Rancho Relaxo as I now call our new home. I get tummy rubs, back massages, comb-outs and reiki. It's so deeply relaxing and I always fall asleep and snore loudly while the Woman is massaging my paws during doggy reiki. She recorded it on her mobile phone and then played it back to me.

The snoring noise was quite alarming, like someone scraping something, but Chiquita said, "See! That's you! That's how noisy you sound when you are sleeping next to me and I have to move baskets to get away from you."

Movie night

It's still raining. It has rained every day and I hate it when we have to sniff around wet leaves and mud. I was watching the television this morning and the weather man said we would get some respite from the soggy conditions.

We explored a new part of the park this morning and met many new dogs. I particularly liked two Wheaten Terriers named Romeo and Devon. They were so well behaved that we felt ashamed at all the yapping and noise we were making. They both looked very healthy, like they worked out every day. Romeo said, "Not really, but we are out in the park from 7.30 a.m. until 9.0 a.m. Our main exercise comes from squirrel hunting. Haven't caught one yet, but I will, believe me, I will." They have a lovely mum who makes them special treats. We rush to her wherever she is in the park. We can spot her a mile off. The lure of those liver treats is just too much. We met another Wheaten – I think his name is Morris – who was being dragged on a lead by an angry-looking owner. He said, "She's pissed off because when I get bored I head off home without her. I like an element of danger in my life, so dodging traffic and people trying to catch me gets the adrenalin going. I always sit on the doorstep and wait for her. When she gets home, she looks well and truly hacked off. She always says the same thing: 'You could have got killed, you stupid effing dog.' No amount of butt wiggling and kissing her makes her calm down.

"I live near a mosque and the worshippers see me coming and usually throw me food as I rush past them. That pisses off my owner even more. There are days when I really am 'in the doghouse', as the saying goes. I hate it when she gives me the cold shoulder."

It's Friday night and the Woman says it's movie night. We can choose from *Harry Pawter*, *The Woof of Wall Street*, *Lord of the Fleas*, *The Dog Father*, *Pup Fiction* (Harry says that's very violent), *The Beagle Has Landed* (Harry likes that one), and *Lady and the Tramp*. Personally, I like watching anything with Brad Pitbull or Woofy Allen's latest film. Choose one now. We all looked at the picture on the cover of the DVD and I said to Pippa, "That's exactly like you. Look, those big, brown, limpid eyes and that lovely glamorous hairstyle." She looked really pleased and said: "Yeah, it does look a bit like me, but I don't go for mangy-looking mutts like that one in the pictures." Woman said we could have Schmackoos as a treat while watching the films. She said, "No Pupcorn, as it sticks in your throat and makes you cough and splutter." I am really looking forward to movie night. Harry said, "I'll watch anything that features a bone and I don't really care who dies in a movie, as long as the dog lives."

Getting rid of foxes

There are lots of wild foxes in the area and every night they scream and yip looking for food. The noises they make are quite scary. If it's not too late at night, the Woman lets us out into the garden and it's wonderful to try and catch the foxes. Usually all of us barking and making a lot of noise chases them away. Greybeard says one good deterrent is for human males to piss everywhere. Trouble is, human males can't piddle on cue like the lads in our pack. Once they have done it, it takes a long time for them to get the urge to piddle again. Dogs have an endless supply of piddle to call on when needed.

Pippa has a new trick that drives us all crazy. After her meal, she picks up her metal bowl and hurls it across the room until the Woman picks it up and puts it out of reach. The noise is very irritating. Pippa says, "It keeps me amused. You never know, we may all get a treat. Then you can thank me."

Talking about irritating, we were discussing what really gets us is when we get dragged away from a deliciously foul stink that could be wonderful to roll in. Harry said, "Don't you just hate it when a toy you are playing with gets stuck under the sofa?" I said, "I bark at the TV when I see dogs and horses on the screen," and Pippa said, "I hate it when another dog (not any of you) wants to share my toy or treat."

Sunday morning coffee and croissant with the park gang

What a lovely way to start our Sunday morning walk. We were invited to have coffee and croissants in the coffee shop with George, a shaggy Jack Russell with anger management issues; Flo, the tiniest little wire-haired Dachshund and her elderly sister, Clemmie. Clemmie always says, "Don't mess with me, Bozo, I've been there, done that and got many T-shirts to prove it." Flo threw herself on her back so that we could sniff her bottom. She then got so excited that she did a fast zoomie around the tables, much to the amusement of all the passing tourists. She really is very cute. She reminds me of a small soft toy. Luckily, we were all kept on leads because we made as much noise as we could every time a dog passed by. All passing dogs got the gang's full blast of yapping and straining-at-the-leads treatment. There was a Weimaraner who stopped to say hello, but he got nervous because we all ganged up on him. He stood still like a statue with his ears right back, and said, "God! You lot are scary!" The humans said we were just a mean, nasty lot. We decided to continue with our walk, and it was really busy meeting many dogs that never get out except at weekends. We played tag with lots of other dogs; got loads of treats from people and by the time we got back to the car, we were all ready for breakfast and a good long nap all day until dinner-time.

Oh! Happy day

This morning was a very happy day for Chiquita and me. We met Chai Latte, our bestest best friend, who we lived with for several months until we were adopted by Greybeard and the Woman. Tita and I always talk of those days fondly. Anyway, Chiquita screamed with excitement, I did leapees in the air and also screamed. I have never felt so animated. Then we both set off on a combined zoomie. Everyone stood by and said, "Wha?

Whoa! What's happening?" It was such a great feeling to meet up with a really good friend.

This evening we went for our walk past the zoo and saw some very unusual creatures. A tiger was lounging on a tree and the keeper jokingly said, "He is considering which one of you dogs would make a nice snack." Then we saw the camels named Naomi and Ghengis, who were chewing grass but didn't show much interest in us even though we went right up to the fence and barked loudly at them. Ghengis stopped chewing and said, "Naff off, you fleabag. All you lot that walk past every day are all mouth and no trousers. Barking at us doesn't scare us." The lions started roaring and that made us all stop and listen. I have never heard a sound like that. It was a scary sound, as though the lions all had a bad sore throat.

It was much more fun to chase the seagulls on the cricket pitch. Harry and Pippa are tied together so that Pippa doesn't do her usual trick of slipping through the railings. Poor old Harry always says, "Oh! Here we go again" and rolls his eyes every day when the lead is clipped on, because he knows he will be dragging her one way and she will be pulling the other way. He says, "I feel like a push-me-pull-you toy." It was beginning to get dark and many tourists were getting tripped up on Harry and Pippa's joint lead. It was very funny to see people leaping over them. The Woman will definitely have to put a flashing light on the lead to alert people and other dogs. Cyclists hate the double lead most of all, as they get their bicycles tangled in it.

Meeting old mates

We sent a couple of hours last night with a gorgeous black Labrador named Roddy, and his brothers, Tristan and Ernie. Tris is a Shih Tzu and gets quite defensive when people refer to him as a "Shit Zu" instead of a "She Zoo".

Ernie is a Standard wirehaired Dachshund, who has to wear a muzzle because of his disgusting eating habits and because he tends to nip other dogs. A few years ago, a bolshy little council-house mongrel raced past him and yelled "Kraut". He went mad and drew lots of blood by really savaging the other mutt, who had to have stitches. It cost his owners a lot of money in vet's bills. I do like Ernie, but I am a little put off by his penchant for eating poo – anyone's poo, he is not fussy. I found that to be quite gross. "Do you think he is perverted?" asked Chiquita. I told her, "No, it isn't a perversion, as I sometimes get a taste for having a munch on your poo. Woman said it could be a lack of vitamins in our diets. Tris said he was adopted by the family of Roddy and Ernie because he lived with the grandmother who became very old and had to go into a home for retired dog owners. He likes Greybeard and the Woman because they were very kind to him in the early days. He used to bite people a lot and they were patient and would explain why it wasn't a nice thing to do. Most people would have shouted and hit him, but not Greybeard. He has such a nice voice."

Roddy is wonderful. He is big and macho, very gentlemanly and doesn't have a bad bone in his body. He has chronic arthritis and is not allowed to chase balls anymore. He curled up on one of the many beds in the house and invited me to curl up beside him. He was so warm and cuddly, and he did smell nice. Chiquita thinks that he is wonderful and loves to snuggle up to him. She says, "I am going to tell Greybeard how nice Roddy is."

Tristy, Ernie and Roddy are very envious of our lifestyle because we are allowed to run free in the park; they said they don't get to walk at all in the afternoons, as the dog walker sits on a bench and talks on the phone for a long time. "Ah, well," they said, "at least we get out of the house." I told them that I had seen them sitting looking sad. "I wish that I could do something to cheer you up," I told them.

Getting stuck in the railings

Our evening walk was quite eventful. We were walking back to the car when Chiquita decided to take a short cut through the railings. We all yelled, "Go back! You won't get through. Don't be stupid, the gap is too narrow," but no! Chiquita tried to prove us wrong and, horror of horrors, she got well and truly stuck, and started struggling and screaming. I ran back to try and help but couldn't shift her. The Woman said some swear words, put us all in the car, then went back to get Chiquita out. She screamed and struggled and tried to bite the Woman, but she finally got pulled out. She was yelling, "Ow! that hurts. Ow! Ow!" When she got into the car, she glared at all of us and said it was the Woman's fault for not putting her on a lead. Pippa said, "Let's face it, you've become a chubby little Costa Rican cutie." Chiquita got really huffy about this and said, "You can talk." We went home and checked in the mirror and she was pleased to see that she looked okay. Nothing looks big on my bum, that's for sure.

It hasn't been a good afternoon for any of us. First it was the chubby-Costa-Rican-stuck-to-the-railings episode, then when we arrived home I climbed onto a chair and managed to drag a box of treats off a shelf. I was very generous and said, "Help ourselves. God put them there so that we could have a munch." There weren't many in the packet, but we forgot to ask Pippa to shred the evidence. When the Woman came into the room, she went ballistic and screamed, "Who did that? C'mon, own up, which one of you took that box off the shelf? Which one was it? Was it you? Or you? Or you?" The others all felt guilty, but the Woman immediately knew it was me and I got the telling off. I took it in the right spirit and said, "Thanks guys! Remind me to do the same for you one day." It was decided that it would be wise to be quiet and take to our beds.

We were all lounging around on the heated kitchen floor watching something called a Pre-Election Debate on television. It was two strange-looking men saying blah! blah! blah! Greybeard asked us who we would vote for. I said, "All I want is to lie on my back and have my tummy tickled many times a day." Greybeard said, "Nice to see that you have got your priorities right." We wouldn't have chosen that programme to watch. We all agreed that *One Man and His Dog* would have been more interesting. Those lovely hunky collies working flat out to get sheep into a pen without losing any of them. That appeals to a dog, definitely. Greybeard suddenly said, "Anyone fancy a ride to the supermarket with me?", so we all jumped up and started getting excited. Greybeard said, "Shaggy can be the chauffeur as usual. He can stand in the middle armrest and I must admit he is a good safe, driver." I get quite huffy, though, when the others start barking at passing dogs. I yell, "Please! Stop with the noise. It's not safe. It's very distracting when you lot start yapping and whining when you see dogs on the street. It's yobbish to start yelling, 'Hey you, your mother was a mongrel' or 'Go back to the shelter that you came from.'"

My new jobs

I am now fully employed. I am security guard, personal trainer, bed warmer and squirrel chaser. Before, I was just a rich pooch with playboy tendencies. We sit in the car and watch the world going by. Some people stop to stare at us looking out at them and making waving signs. When we start barking, I always say, "Please people, let's behave with decorum."

Tiverton Green

Yawn. It's Saturday. Aside from being another day of my having to be charming, cuddly, adorable, waggy and sweet, I wondered what surprise Greybeard and Woman had in store for us.

We went to Tiverton Green this afternoon, a small park known as Dog Shit Alley because no one picks up after their dogs. However, each poo holds a message for the rest of us, so it was quite an interesting afternoon walk. We spent half an hour going from message to

message. A lot of Eastern European dogs visit this park. There was an aggressive message from Vladimir, a Siberian Husky, who was up for a fight with any dog off the lead. The message was: "I'm lean, mean and others don't stand a chance." Ooooh, scary! Dogs like that can tear you limb from limb. Woman said, "I don't really like this park, it's too scruffy," but we all said in unison, "We do. We do! It's full of interesting smells."

We had sardines and pellets for supper. I don't think I had ever tasted sardines before, but I can tell you that they were lip-smackingly good and I wouldn't mind them again. Maybe the Woman will give them to us again.

Harry and Pippa are going home to Chiswick tomorrow. I've had great fun with Pippa. In a way, I will miss Harry's gloomy lectures. He means well. Eric, the Chihuahua, came for the day. He often comes for doggy day care because his people work in television and don't get home until late at night. Eric says, "I don't mind coming for doggy day care, as it means I am not sitting in the dark waiting for them to come home." I asked him if it's a lonely life and he said, "I'm used to it. I graze a lot, as they leave food and water down so that

I can eat whenever I like. Do you think I look porky or can I blame it on the new collar?" I reassured him that he was a smart lean little lad.

Greybeard loves opera, so I am lying at his feet listening to Pupcini. It's quite sad and I think I prefer the Brazilian jazz that the Woman likes listening to. You can wag your tail in time to that. My taste is more musical: I prefer Lionel Itchy, Barry Mangypaws and Stink, just to name three of my favourite artistes. Woman sometimes plays a special CD that is for animals. Now that is very soothing and it makes us all fall into a deep sleep. No twitching, grunting or yipping goes on. Chiquita says that I sound like a tractor when I snore. Huh! She sometimes thinks she is the perfect Bichon. I've got news for her.

Pawty time when the folks are out

Greybeard and the Woman went out shopping and left us alone in the house. They said, "Be good, all of you, and look after the house. We'll be back soon." I don't know how it happened, but one of the gang started racing up and down the stairs like a mad thing having a zoomie, so we all joined in rushing up and down. Then suddenly there was a crash and lots of things got broken. Greybeard and Woman came home unexpectedly and screamed, "O my god! It looks like a bomb has gone off. What have you done?" When the accident happened, we said to Chiquita, "You're the favourite, so you do the whole bum wriggle, talking and looking sweet bit." Chiquita was brilliant. She made a big fuss of Greybeard, jumping all over him, kissing him and telling him, "I'm really glad you've come home, because it was very scary. That big plant suddenly just fainted and fell out of its pot." The Woman looked very chilly and started to clear up the mud and broken bits of the plant. Then she said, "Before you guys piss me off again, remember, I may seem really nice and easy going, but I can go from 1 to level 100 of crazy in under 60 seconds. You are all under notice from now on to behave yourselves." We looked at each other and I said, "Ooops! Time to hide and be good," and that's what we did for the rest of the day. You could have cut the atmosphere with a knife. The others all whispered, "No treats tonight then!"

We all feel flat and deflated today as Harry and Pippa went home. I will really miss little Pippa and the mischief that she made us all get up to. The house is very quiet and although we went for our evening walk, it wasn't the same as the whole gang chasing squirrels and magpies. Pippa said, "Let's stay in touch," but everyone says that, don't they? I expect I won't see any of my lovely friends again, but I am sure I will make new ones.

A woman in the park was admiring Chiquita and me, and she said to the Woman, "The good thing about dogs is that their love is completely unconditional." I whispered sarcastically, "She can believe anything she likes, but just keep on dishing out treats, scratching behind the ears, the tummy or anywhere else and we will do anything that you ask."

I just wanna be a dog

I woke up this morning and thought to myself, "I don't want to be adult today. I don't even want to be human. I just want to be a dog. I will be stretched out on the floor. Please pet me and bring me treats."

"Get you," said Chiquita, "the moment you catch fleas and you pass one to Greybeard, they won't be giving you the little prince treatment." My sister may be cute and nice, but she does have a way of bringing you down to earth.

It has rained all day. We went for our evening walk togged up in waterproof gear with flashing lights. I hate these coats and harnesses, so I decided to play up by giving the Woman a run for her money. "Watch this," I told my sister. Instead of staying in one place doing my poo in one spot, I moved several times so that poor

Woman had to search in the rain. "That's a mean thing to do," said Chiquita. I wanted that coat off, so I rubbed himself on trees; it came off, but was still hanging from my neck. Woman got irritated and snatched the coat off me. "Anyone else want to play up?" she asked.

Billy No Mates

A new member of the gang arrived to stay for a few days while his owners attend bridge championships in Paris. He introduced himself as Billy, or, as I whispered to myself, "Billy No Mates", because he does have chronic bad breath. Poor boy! Needs some dental work done. Ask Chiquita about it. He tried to kiss her and she said it was like having a compost heap smothering her. Sweet boy, but a tad overweight. He uses his lounging around in his bed as the reason for looking chubby and then says, "But I do like my food" and laughs. We got on well and I think I will enjoy having chats with him about many things. He was very interested in knowing about me, my pedigree, my family background and my likes and dislikes. Shows he is *sympatico* to others and not just in cadging gravy bones from people in the park. I think Chiquita and I will be counting on him as a good friend. Not a mean bone in his body. He seems to know a lot about bridge and chess. He says he can gaze at a table top for hours.

Chiquita and I have been hauled off to the grooming parlour, as we looked as though we had been dragged through a hedge backwards. Mind you, we did have the most wonderful time chasing squirrels and birds in a wooded area of the park this morning. We stalked as many as we could and were joined by a Whippet, a Spaniel, a Westie and some mongrels. We have arranged to meet up tomorrow morning and do the same exercise. We all agreed it was such fun. We were the heroic bunch of hunters in the forest! We scent! We locate! We stalk! We attack! And then we found the discarded pizza boxes in the undergrowth and all of us started licking the leftovers in them. Woman and the other owners shrieked and screamed for us to stop and come back. I said to Billy, "What is their problem? The boxes were empty anyway."

Back from the groomers looking clean, fluffed up and smelling positively ridiculous. I immediately ran into the garden and rolled in a wet flowerbed, much to the Woman's anguish. "Ah, well," she said, "you can't force him to be pristine and smelling of doggy cologne." She is very sanguine about what we do. I told Billy that our lives before had been very restrictive."We were adored but never let off the lead, so you can imagine how much we enjoy the freedom of doing what we want, when we want." Chiquita said, "Yeah, but don't take advantage of her kind nature, will you? I think she is wonderful."

The gang's all back

Guess what? Today is fun Friday. Jimmy is back for the weekend, as moody as ever, and Marnie arrived half an hour ago saying, "Hi, gang! I'm back. Let the party begin." The two squirrels that were munching peanuts and sitting on our fence got the shock of their lives when Marnie said, "Let's go get 'em!" and five of us rushed out making as much noise as we could.

I feel in my paws that this is going to be an action-packed weekend. No more lying around on the floor asking each other what the point of life is. Are we here for a reason? Jimmy said that we do have a point to our existence and that it is to lie on the floor and get in everybody's way. He says his favourite spot is right in the middle of the kitchen floor because the humans all yell, "MOVE, damn you!" Chiquita says her favourite place to stretch out is on the third step, so that the humans have to negotiate a way down.

My duties as co-driver

We drove to the park. I take my duties very seriously and when the others start shouting, "Yah! Boo! Hiss!" and yelling nasty names at dogs on leads walking along the street, I get very tight lipped and say, "Stop, you lot! It's very nasty to start calling other dogs names and jeering 'Ah! your mother was a mongrel.' That's anti-dogist. It wlll be our bad luck to meet them as we get out at the park gates. I'm not in the mood for a bit of fur pulling. I know Marnie is up for it, but the rest of you wimps will be hiding behind us, saying, 'Hit him! Go on, hit him! Here, let me hold your coat.' So stop, okay? It's very distracting!"

Mind you, after that lecture, I jumped out of the car, turned to look at the others with a wicked grin and said, "Watch this!" There were two women in long black dresses strolling along the path and I suddenly lunged at them, barking furiously. They screamed and ran in different directions, looking very frightened. The Woman was shouting at me, "Come back at once, now, this instant! How dare you attack people!" I said, "I Iove doing that. It gets the adrenalin going and sets me up for the day."

We spent the next hour chasing seagulls, magpies and pigeons.

On our way out we stopped to exchange butt sniffs with three gorgeous
Golden Retrievers, with their tails
going swish! swish! swish! Marnie had
first go, but said that all that swishing
made them high and mighty. Then I
heard the puppy among them asking, "Mummy, why are they making

remarks and laughing" and she said, "Ignore them,
sweetie, it's just tail envy!"

We met lots and lots of dogs, some sniffing at us, some
snarling because they were on a lead. Suddenly Jimmy
got into a mood and started galloping for the car. We
all yelled at him to come back, but he said "Nah! Too
many close encounters for my liking." I wonder why
we all turn into *Cujo* – fierce, loud, aggressive snarl-
heads when we are on leads. Off the leads, we have no
problem meeting others, but once that lead goes on,
it's "Watch out." When we arrived home, the Woman
said, "Shaggy, you and I need to have an owner-to-dog
heart-to-heart about your appalling behaviour these
last few weeks." Marnie said to the others, "Oh! Lord,
he is going to get both barrels now."

I sat with the Woman on the stairs and she told me that
she was very disappointed at my recent behaviour. She
felt that I was getting overconfident. I was becoming
disobedient, aggressive towards other dogs on leads,

chasing joggers, eating rubbish in the park, climbing on the dining table when her back was turned to find food, and she was very unhappy with me. I gazed into her eyes, put on my most sincere expression and promised I would change. I put my head on her shoulder and my paw in her lap. I snuck a look at the others, winked and said, "How am I doing?"

The Woman went on to say, "If you continue to push the envelope and misbehave, I will have to stop all your privileges and you will be put on a retractable lead". Then she looked at each one of the others and said, "And that goes for the rest of you too." I went down the stairs and settled into a bed under the table. Marnie said, "I'm off to the TV room." Chiquita complained, "The rest of us haven't done anything so why are we going to be punished?"

My many names

I have discovered that I have many names and these are the ones most frequently used.
Shaggy! get off the table!
Shaggy! drop it!
Shaggy! I am serious. Drop it!
Shaggy! be gentle!
Shaggy! stop shouting!
Shaggy! No, down, shut-the-f…-up!

Shaggy! what are you doing now?
SHAGGY! stop licking your balls!
S- H- A- G- G -Y! Stop that will you!
Shaggy! What the f… did you roll in now? In the shower you go when we get home.

My Christmas carol

The Woman has just put up a very pretty green round thing on the door. She let me sniff it and told me, "That's a Christmas wreath. It goes up once a year, but after the 26th of December, it starts to looks tatty. Did you celebrate Christmas, Chiquita and Shaggy?" I said I didn't know, as one day feels just like any other to me. She said, "All dogs in this family get a special dinner and a present." She said having us come to live with them was the best Christmas present ever. I thought that was the nicest thing to say. She taught us the words to a Christmas carol. I will sing it to you when you come to visit Greybeard and the Woman.

Four birds falling!
3 dead squirrels!
2 squeaky toys!
and a long pee on a short tree!

Today I taught the gang the art of manipulation. You place your chin on your owner's knee and look up at them with big, sad eyes and I guarantee that you will be given a cuddle and a treat. Easy peasy!

I've got the Woman beautifully trained. When she is making a sandwich for herself, she gives me a tiny bit. I then jump onto the sofa, she follows with her plate of food and settles down to eat. I sit in front and start dribbling. She gives me another bit, then she gives me a big kiss on the top of my head and a cuddle. Yup! I'd say I've got her pretty well trained.

What is this Christmas?

How was Christmas for you? I have no idea what it was. Is it the same as *Feliz Navidog* in Spanish? But it felt special. Greybeard and Woman made sure that we had a good time. We went everywhere with them. They dressed my sister and me in red bows, and everywhere we went, people cooed at us and stopped to pet us. I could get used to all this attention. Harry, the one who knows it all, gave us some good advice before we went visiting others' homes. He told us to sit by children, as they always feed you titbits and the younger ones drop food. He also told us to stay away from old people, as they fart when they snooze and you will get the blame.

We acted as security guards at every house we visited. We sniffed every visitor and their bags as they came through the door. Each house that we went to was full of wrapped presents under a tree with many lights. We had great fun sniffing around the piles. Aftershave… socks… wallet… chocolates… yay! I've found a doggie present. A rubber chicken and a tennis ball, plus a box of gravy bones. "Look how smart they are," said the humans.

Rasmus, the Danish-speaking Bichon, very kindly gave each one of us sticks for Christmas that he had carefully selected and picked up in the park. He told us that he had kept a note of the locations in case we wanted to exchange them. I told him, "No branch is ever too small or too big." I notice that some dogs pick up tree trunks in the park and call themselves branch managers.

I don't mind the new Christmas collar, but I am not too sure about the antlers or the red hat with a bell. I feel that it's beneath any dog's dignity to be dressed up as a pawty piece. Mind you, it's better to go with the flow and not get too fussed about looking like a dog's breakfast.

The woodland walk

Thank god, we woke up to a nice sunny day without rain. We have been going for walks in rain every day and I can tell you, it is a real pain, as the wet mud gets into our paws. I hate dirty paws and can't wait to get home, have breakfast and clean my feet.

We have spent a long time sniffing the garden today. Next door's cat was sitting on the fence watching us. We screamed and barked at him. He said, "Chill, guys. I can't let you chase me, as I am under house arrest." We asked why and he told us, "I became addicted to catnip and to fund my habit, I took to stalking and performing perverted and sadistic acts on the neighbourhood squirrels and birds. Now I have to wear a damned bell to alert the world." I was very sympathethic to his plight and told him that we would stop barking and chasing him along the fence. I asked, "Is there anything we can do for you? You are quite welcome to sunbathe on our shed any time you like." That made the cat well up and he said, "No one ever says nice things to me any more. I really appreciate your friendship."

I love the way that the Woman always shows us her hands when she has stopped eating something. She told us that she feels like a blackjack dealer each time she does it.

We all looked at each other and asked, "What is a blackjack dealer?" Harry, who is the oldest and most knowledgeable of us, said, "I think it is something to do with rubber balls or gravy bones." He was given an iPeed as a Christmas present, and now he is obsessed with sniffing the same places to find out if someone has peed over his pee.

We went to a new part of the park, known as the Woodland Walk. It was wonderful. It was full of trees and bushes and shrubs. We scurried around in different directions, getting lost. Poor Woman did look really cold, so we all decided to poo close to each other so that she could warm up her hands by picking up hot poo.

ASBO for dogs

Manchas came back for a few days. I can tell you that dog is a maniac. He climbs trees, as you know, but now he has started tearing the bark off them. A park keeper stopped him and said, "Oy! you little vandal! Stop that at once!", but Manchas is so obsessed that he didn't pay any attention. The park keeper was very cross and gave the Woman a long lecture on how trees can be killed by Manchas stripping the bark. He issued her with an official warning and the recommendation that Manchas wears a muzzle. ASBO Manchas now wears a soft muzzle and sits in a cage in the boot of the car. At every journey to the park, he sings, "I'm a prisoner! Get me outta here." Chiquita hates him for being such a loudmouth, and you know something, I agree with her. He really can be a yob! He does keep us amused, though, because he is the only dog I have met who can catch his tail while going around in circles and at the same time farting. He thinks it is really amusing, but not when he does it all the time. His philosophy is that only when someone catches their tail, can one fully understand the circle of life.

I do love Greybeard and the Woman because they talk to us all the time. They apologise if they step on us, say goodbye when they go out, and say "Excuse me" when they want to go past. They always say good morning, hello, please and thank you. Their courtesy is so infectious that I find myself treating others in the same way. They say manners maketh the man… or, in my case, the Dog.

Beyoncé – no not that one!

A beautiful miniature Dachshund came to stay for a few days. She was tiny, like a toy, with beautiful markings. She shyly told us her name was Beyoncé. "*Beyoncé!*" we all yelped. "That's not a dog's name." She said to blame it on the teenage children who named her as a puppy. She was a gutsy little girl, game for anything and if anyone looked aggressively at any of us, she was in there ready for a punch-up. We all called her Bea and looked out for her in the park. Being so small, she sometimes gets knocked for six by a big dog, but boy, oh boy, what a foghorn bark for such a tiny dog. (That's what Greybeard said, because I have no idea what a foghorn is.)

We all were very protective of Bea. She loved to spend every day with Greybeard in his office. We teased her and asked her if this was her holiday romance. I loved it that Chiquita and I immediately made her feel welcome and part of the gang. She was another fluent Spanish speaker, so we would chatter away together. It was wonderful, because we could say nasty things about other dogs in the park and they had no idea that we were being rude about them. We are quite a multilingual group.

What not to do with the TV remote

We were watching television with Greybeard, all snuggled up in blankets. Then, suddenly, oops! Rasmus, who should speak fluent Danish but doesn't, put his paw on the remote and changed the programme. Greybeard told him not to get overconfident. When we had settled down again for a snooze, Greybeard tried to open a box of chocolates quietly. Tell you what? Humans are definitely not good at opening sweet bags silently. I can hear a sweet bag opening from the next room even if I am in a deep sleep. We all leapt up and crowded around him.

Herbie, the little Norfolk Terrier, told us the sad news that his brother, Alfie, had died of old age, but he said the joy of now being an only child is that he gets a lot of quality time with Mummy and Daddy or Daddy or Mummy. We told him he would start looking like a brown pudding if he carried on scrounging for treats. He said his dad is a real sucker for the I-am-starving-look and that's guaranteed to get a treat. He told us that it was really sad when his elderly brother went to Rainbow Bridge, as he was unwell for quite a long time. Greybeard and the Woman were very fond of Alfie and treated him like their own.

We go to bed when the Woman tidies up the kitch-en and starts climbing the stairs. Each one of us has a comfy basket to sleep in, but we jump on the bed and wait for her to climb in. But the moment we hear Greybeard's footsteps climbing the stairs, we spread out so that he has to fight for a space on the bed. Every night he bellows, "Off! Move! Go to your own baskets. This bed is for humans." We reluctantly get off the bed, but when they are both asleep, we quietly climb back on and snuggle up to them.

Farmyard adventures

Today was different to our normal going-to-the-park day. We drove for a long time and arrived at a place that Greybeard called a farm. There were many strange-looking birds and animals. We were lectured on what to do and what not to do. No barking at the horses or cows, no chasing the chickens and the sheep, but we could go and sniff in that field. It was a pick-and-roll cow-pat farm. I rolled in one that was beautifully fresh and moist. Chiquita found one that was dry and crispy. "That's what I am." she said, "a dry and crispy girl!" Getting dunked in the bath made the day worth all that stinky rolling. I even sampled some fresh horse poo. The humans said that it was fresh vegetarian food and wouldn't do me any harm but it was not recommended as a daily diet. We told Greybeard that it was the best day we have ever had. "Good!" he said, "Nice to see you both so happy."

The Woman asked me why I trembled so much in the garden or park. The vet told her that all dogs tremble from head to paw when watching squirrels, cats, and birds, even if they are locked indoors. It's excitement. So that's okay, then.

Tonight we were dozing on the sofa with Greybeard, watching *Canine Mastermind* on TV, when the quizmaster asked the Golden Retriever, "And what is your specialist subject, Ricky?" Ricky answered, "Sweeping things off coffee tables with my tail." I thought that was good.

At the park today, the Woman got quite irate and asked us, "Why do these bloody people hang bags of poo on the railings?" We said that we couldn't answer that question, as it was never discussed at Puppy University. "And look," she ranted, "the new pollution is discarded gloves and masks. Why are people so lazy? All they have to do is take it home and put it in a bin." Personally, we dogs would solve the problem by just ripping the bags open for others to sniff, pee on them and sometimes roll in it. And that would be the end of it.

I lurve sticks

It's very quiet today. "Hey, gang! Great news! I think they had a late night and are suffering hangovers. Brilliant! One of you do the squeaky toy thing. Chiquita and I will do the barking at the pretend squirrel in the garden, and everyone else can bark at an imaginary knock on the door. Irritating or what?"

When we were out, I picked up a long stick to take back to the car and the Woman was in a bad mood and yelled at me, "For Pete's sake! Can't we just have a simple walk without you dragging back an entire forest? Leave it, leave it! There's no more room in the car for junk."

That reminds me, one of our doggy guests, I can't remember who, gave us sticks as presents. He said, "I've kept the location in case you want to take it back." Oh! Yes! I remember now, it was Rasmus, who speaks fluent Hubliaki (Danish rubbish). Well, that's what it sounds like.

Some good books for us dogs to read:

- *How to Give Humans the Illusion of Being In Charge*
- *The Joys of Nocturnal Barking*
- *Squirrel Watching Without Excessive Trembling and Dribbling*
- *100 Ways to Make Your Owners Feel Guilty*
- *Effective Begging*
- *How to Make Their Bed Your Bed*
- *The Art of the Silent-But-Deadly Fart*
- *How to Avoid the Vet*
- *100 Ways to Get More Treats*
- *The Guilty Pleasures of Rolling In Fox Poo*
- *The Art of Throwing Your Food Around*
- *Swimming in Muddy Puddles*

Don't you just hate it when they do that?

I do wish the Woman would stop cutting treats in half. We are not idiots and we know when we are getting half measures.

Other things that I hate are when they pretend to throw the ball; say "TREATS!" to trick me to do something or to go outside; blame me for their farts; and stop me from rolling in something.

The Woman was cuddling us while we were sitting on the stairs. I asked her, "Can you please tell me again the story of how you adopted Chiquita and me?" She did, and she told us that we were the best things to happen to her and Greybeard. That made us feel really happy, as we aim to please. It gave me such a warm feeling.

I remember Nick, the lovely man at the Grand Union Pets Grooming Parlour, telling everyone that finding Greybeard and the Woman to adopt us was a match made in heaven. He has known us since we were *kleine kinder* puppies, as they say in Doglish.

The full-on dog owning look

The Woman has definitely got her full-on dog look today. She has our leashes draped round her neck, dog hairs all over her coat and muddy paw prints on her trousers. The whistle, which we completely ignore but makes her feel in control and, of course, the bag of treats in a little bag are all hanging off her neck. She needs just one essential accessory: the brightly-coloured little poo bags tied to one of the leads.

A Springer Spaniel has come to stay for a week. I can't remember his name. He is a sweet guy but he is totally wearing us out. He is high energy and drooling all the time. It's driving me nuts and none of us are getting the chance to snooze, and I'm beginning to comfort eat anything I can find on the floor. Why did the Woman agree to look after him for one week? I can't wait for him to go home. The Woman said, "Springer Spaniels are definitely decaff, as they are so hyper." I meant to ask her what decaff means. I still don't know what it means.

I got yelled at this morning for chasing a man who was dressed like a condom riding a bike through the park. I don't know what a condom is, but I heard another human describe the clothes that way. Another dog owner snitched on me and told the Woman that I was chasing a man on a bike. I said, "Huh! She's got it wrong. I don't even own a bike and besides I wasn't chasing him but racing him."

There was Greybeard slumped in front of the television, so I sat in front of him and put out the thought "I need a cuddle." I then gave him the big, sad eyes... the hopeful flick of the tail... the irresistible head to one side... then the soft, pathetic whimper... followed by the paw on the knee and a small yap of desperation. Then, as none of those moves were working, I changed tack: I jumped onto his lap and started slobbering kisses on his face, and said, "Gimme a cuddle, damn you!" That worked.

"Go on, dogs! Fetch the stick," the Woman said because she thinks we don't get enough exercise. Henry, the Dachshund, said, "Don't move a muscle. My dad's a lawyer and he would tell you that the stick doesn't comply with health and safety guidelines on stick weight, length and volume. There are also health and safety rules about getting splinters in your mouth."

The Riot Act

Today the Woman read us the Riot Act for jumping out of the car and chasing a moggy who was casually strolling down the street like he owned it. Woman shouted, "I don't care how many cute and funny videos of dogs chasing cats you've seen on YouTube, you do not chase them when you are living with us." Shame! It was such fun watching that cat take off like a rocket.

Puppy love

A friend of Greybeard and the Woman has just got a puppy. Friend brought puppy over to introduce it to us. They kept saying, "Be nice! Be nice!" Chiquita says it sounded like: "Brr! Numm! Brr! Numm!" Humans don't realize that when they are talking to us dogs, we don't really understand their dialect but pretend that we do. That makes them very happy because they think we are very intelligent and know exactly what they are saying. Hah!

Puppy was a cute little thing and smelled warm and toasty. We sniffed it, rolled it over onto its back, stuck our tongues into its ears and tried to get it to play, but it decided to pee instead, then fell asleep.

Luckily, we have wooden floors, otherwise it would have got told off. Everybody else gets yelled at if we lift our legs. I grew up hearing, "DON'T YOU DARE LIFT YOUR LEG IN THE HOUSE!"

I think Puppy is going to be named "Eats, sleeps and craps". Before the puppy went home, we gave it some useful tips on riding in the car.

1. The moment the car starts to move, start panting heavily. This is a good way to make them nervous. They then put you on their lap.

2. Wipe your nose and saliva on the window.
3. Whimper excitedly.
4. As the car gets nearer to home, start yelping loudly as if you are in pain.
5. As soon as you get out of the car, pee immediately.
6. If you see another dog, go demented and start yapping and barking.
7. The moment you get indoors, fall asleep on the floor.
8. Wake up after 10 minutes and do a fart. Phwoar! That's one of the things they will teach you at puppy school: "Never waste a fart in the open air – always do it in the car or in the house."

Brass monkeys means?

Boy, it was cold this morning. Harry said it was cold enough to freeze the balls off a brass monkey. We asked, "What is a brass monkey? How would you know?" But he just tapped the side of his nose with his paw. I wanted to ask Greybeard what the saying meant, but I don't think he would know. Harry knows it all and he has his reasons for saying it.

Psychic paw readings

The Woman was sorting through a drawer and found a pack of tarot cards and explained to us what they were for. She asked, "Okay, Who wants a psychic paw reading? Who wants to be first?" Pippa jumped up and down and yipped, "Me! Me! I want to be first!" The Woman shuffled the cards, turned them over and said to Pip, "I see you becoming a very successful escape artiste, like Houdini. You will be well known for getting in and out of places other dogs can't. You will also be known as the Great Destroyer for chewing shoes, paper and anything that falls on the floor. This will cause your owners great aggravation, especially when you chew and destroy expensive designer shoes. You will enjoy a very pampered life."

Jimmy, the Dachshund, said, "How about me? What do the cards show for me?" Woman shuffled them and looked at one and said, "Your card shows plenty of foreign travel, a change of residence and plenty of hair shedding on the carpet, sofa, stairs and in the car. You will live in the French countryside and go for adventures in the surrounding fields. You will miss London and all your friends, but you are a country boy at heart." Chiquita said, "I don't believe in all that rubbish, as millions of dogs have the same reading. Give me a good bone any day. I like positive things." The Woman said, "How about you, Shags? I'll read your horoscope from today's paper instead of the cards, shall I? You're an Aries, right? It says here, 'You will bark at delivery men several times in the week. You will enjoy many different walks in new places with lots of lovely smells. You might even get to roll in something revolting. By the end of the week you may suffer from an itchy bottom and pay a visit to the vet. Life will be good for you.'"

Manners please

Today I was having a lovely snooze on the sofa when Greybeard walks into the room, hands on hips, and stands there glaring at me and says, "C'mon Shags, off. OFF, I TELL YOU, OFF NOW!" I opened my eyes, looked at him and closed my eyes again.

"I've just got comfortable."

"Off you get!"

"Say please, then I will get off." Sometimes he just doesn't know what courtesy is!

Oh, what a wonderful day it has turned into! Greybeard was talking to a neighbour in the front garden when he suddenly called out, "Shaggy! Chiquita! Come out and see who is here!" We dashed to the front door and saw Auntie Viv and Chai Latte, our bestest and dearest friend, standing on the pavement. We got out from under the gate and had the most exciting reunion. We haven't seen them for months. It was brilliant and we were so. We could tell from the worried looks on the Woman and Greybeard's faces that they thought maybe we wanted to go home with Auntie, but we turned and went back to the house. This really pleased them. Chiquita said to me, "I like the Woman and Greybeard, so why would we want to leave?"

Jealousy

I'm becoming a jealous fur ball. When Greybeard picked up another dog to cuddle, I put my paw on his mouth and said, "I can't bear it when you touch someone else. I don't like sharing you with strangers." Chiquita said, "What are you like, Shags? All this possessiveness is a new thing."

Two white dogs named Penny and Henry are with us for two weeks. Henry has kept us in fits of laughter by saying, "Watch this folks!" Then he walks on his front legs, lifts his back legs and sprays pee everywhere. Very, very funny but the grave danger is that if you stand too close, you get splattered by pee. The tourists love this party trick and take endless photographs. Henry said, "I'm probably on a hundred postcards somewhere in the world."

Penny is a pretty little Maltese Terrier, who told us that her pet hate is the musical *The Sound of Music*. She says the moment she hears "The hills are alive with the sound of music", she takes off and hides under furniture. "I hate it, absolutely hate it. I don't know why, because no one has ever tortured me by holding me down and making me listen to that song."

Tilly, a Terrier, has come to stay for one week. Quite a sweet little thing, but she obviously has a problem, because she says she has to attend weekly self-help therapy sessions with Barkers and Yappers.

She told us that the reason her owners booked her in here with us was because she was totally out of control. Barking at everything and anything – bicycles, joggers, birds, cats, lamp-posts, airplanes, scooters, even clouds. She said, "I desperately wanted to stop but couldn't. I am better now." Chiquita said, "Sounds a bit like you, Shags." I said, "Aw, c'mon, I'm not that bad. I can think of many others who are even worse."

Doesn't take much to make her happy

The Woman was thrilled today because I wrote a little poem especially for her. It read:

> *Roses are red*
> *Violets are blue*
> *Thanks for the tummy rubs*
> *And picking up my poo*

She gave me a big cuddle and said, "That's really nice, Shaggy."

When guests overstay their welcome

The Woman said to Greybeard, "Oh dear! How can we get rid of these people?" Chiquita said, "You know how, let's make them feel really uncomfortable, as they aren't really dog lovers. Okay! Let's do it together. You stick your nose into his crotch and I will sniff her ankles. You watch! She will start crossing her legs." Then she will say, "Heavens! Is that really the time? We must get going, as the poor cat needs feeding."

Why do people say "working like a dog". We don't know any pooches that work. I tell a lie. Everyday day we meet Jasper, Cody, Diesel and all the other police dogs who work as sniffer dogs searching out drugs, guns, explosives and other things at airports and railway stations. One of them was telling me that it's a very disciplined way of life and the only reward they get after completing a task is a tennis ball. We said, "What? No treats?" And they said, "No! Not allowed, in case we get fat and lose the will to work." Chiquita said, "Wouldn't suit you, Shags." Huh! What cheek!

The Woman was cuddling Chiquita and me and saying, "My beautiful darling fur babies. I love you both very much. I can't ever imagine my life without you. Kiss! Kiss!"

Greybeard looked up from his newspaper and said, "Well, kids, she once used to talk to me like that."

A dog's itinerary

Hmmmm! I've got a long list of things to do today:
- Stretch
- Yawn
- Lick my balls
- Have a good noisy scratch
- Go for a walk in the park
- Come back for breakfast
- Rush into the garden and chase off the birds
- Climb into my bed and nap until 4.30 p.m.
- Throw my dish around as a hint for dinner
- Get ready for a walk in the park
- Come home and get ready for bed

That's it! I've done everything on my list.

Rolling in stinky stuff

Did I tell you that I found a dead bird on my walk this morning? It was well dead. Rigor mortis had set in, so I rolled all over it. It was bliss. When we got back to the car, Greybeard shouted, "Crikey, Shaggy, you really stink! You've rolled in something and it's in the shower for you when we get home. Phwoar! You smell disgusting." Humans have no appreciation of the good things in a dog's life.

Poor Chiquita has hurt her paw and is limping badly. It's not broken but Greybeard thinks she probably sprained it or got grass seed in her paw. It was bandaged up but she has been licking it non-stop and that makes it worse. Woman put Manuka honey on it for two days and now Chiquita is much better. I have been licking her paw, too, to make her feel better and I am so glad that I could help.

Chiquita is milking the sympathy vote for all it's worth. The Woman wrapped her paw in a bandage and every time a person came along and said, "Oh! Poor puppy! Have you hurt your paw?", she looked up at them with big eyes and limped. They would give her a treat. Then, as an afterthought, I would get one too. I told Chiquita she was becoming quite the con artist.

How to make your owner uncomfortable

Today in the park, two long-haired Chihuahas tried to hump Chiquita, and there she was limping along, trying to fend them off. Their owner kept saying, "They mean no harm, they only want to play."

There was no way I was going to let them hassle her, so I body bombed one of them. He screamed like a stuck pig and ran off. I heard his owner say, "Serves you right."

Whenever I sit and stare at the Woman – and many times I do it just to let her know how much I love her – she shouts, "What? What is it you want now? Why are you staring at me? The door is open – go chase a squirrel!" But I blink at her several times and she says, "Awww, Shags, what a sweet boy you are!"

The Woman was sitting looking at the TV when she turned to me and said, "For God's sakes, Shaggy, you've been staring at me for over an hour. What's your problem?" So I jumped up, gave her a kiss on the hand and sent her the thought message, "I love you and I am just reminding you of my existence."

That pesky tree rat

That damned squirrel was standing on our lawn, looking grumpy, with its arms crossed, and squeaking loudly: "Covid this... Covid that! The damned bird feeder is still empty, lady! It wouldn't hurt you to fill it up now and again."

"Right! You ungrateful little tree rat. It's about time I taught you a lesson." I whooshed out of that door so fast that it scared the living daylights out of him and he jumped over the fence and vanished. He is a resourceful little rat, so no doubt he will be back scrounging in *my* garden. He never seems to get the message and comes back every day.

Woman says to me, "Go on, Shags! Fetch the ball!"
I said to the gang, "Like, why? Like what's the point? You want me to, like, chase a piece of wet, muddy rubber for your pleasure? I'm not a teenager, y'know! No way, lady! You want that ball, you go fetch it."

The Woman said, "Are we feeling in a bad mood, Shags?"

Lola, the Fox Terrier, came to stay for a few days. She is one of those uptight, mincing, society-type dogs that look good in movies. Very elegant, but hates having her space invaded. She got into hair-yanking sessions with some of the others. She is not averse to biting you because you have annoyed her. Chiquita hates her and whispered to me, "To tell the truth, she scares me." Pippa said, "Don't let her get to you. She's a social misfit who is not used to mixing with us plebby dogs. Just ignore her." Lola then gets upset because we are all ignoring her. I am sure she is really nice once she gets over her hang-ups. She doesn't want to join the gang in rolling, sniffing or playing games. I think she aspires to being a human and prefers them to us.

Little Toby, who is quite elderly, has come to stay for a few days too. He is 15 years old, blind, but very feisty. When we all said "hello", he answered that he prefers to use the word "*Konichiwa*", which is hello in Japanese. He was a sweet old dog, who liked to spend his time in the bathroom but come out for a walk with us on a long lead. Chiquita made him as welcome as she could and he was very appreciative of her kindness. She would stroll with him and they would discuss all sorts of things. She walked alongside him so that he didn't fall down the stairs. Now we can speak Japanese as well as Spanish and French.

Buying Manchas a drone

We were having a dog pow-wow and it was decided that we would pool our bone money and buy Manchas a drone so that he could get to the tree tops to catch squirrels. He thought that was a brill idea, but he didn't think he would have time to go to drone school.

Woman said, "We are going out and won't be back until late, so behave yourselves and don't wreck the house, please." We pretended to look very sad and she gave us all a treat, then the moment we heard the door close and the gate clunk shut, we looked at each other and said, "Let's pawty!" Marnie started off by throwing a cushion up in the air. Jimmy caught it and Henry started a tug of war. Then we all did zoomies up and down three flights of stairs. It was really enjoyable. When Greybeard and the Woman came home, we were pretending to be asleep in our baskets and I heard him say, "They've been very good – I can't see any damage." The next day our neighbour said, "Your dogs had a great pawty while you were out. We could hear them hurtling up and down the stairs."

The best gang in the park

Dum de dum de dum! Our gang are the boss of the park. The mighty gang of dogs. We strike fear into all who see us. Pigeons, crows and seagulls scatter; squirrels rush up trees and out of harm's way; dogs run away whimpering. Oh! Sorry! No, it's the owners who move away when the mighty gang approaches. "Oh! Look there's that black poodle," so we yell "Hello! Mr-nice-much-bigger-than-us-dog."

Ahem! Now then, where were we?

It's raining... pouring with water and the Woman tried to kick us out, but Chiquita said, "No way am I going out in that!" so we sat on the kitchen floor and watched the wildlife playing in the garden. Chiquita looked at me, giggled and said, "C'mon, let's bark loudly at nothing." So we did until the Man with Beard shouted, "Pack it in!"

The stick box

How nice! Some kindly dog owner has built a box by the entrance to the park and put up a notice that says "Stick Library. Help yourself." It was full of sticks of all sizes. I don't think there was a charge but some of the big dogs are being greedy and taking two or three sticks at a time. It's a bit selfish. It makes me chuckle because the really small dogs, like Yorkies and Dachshunds are taking the giant-size sticks, dragging them along the paths. It's a good way to exercise social distancing, as humans have to leap out of the way to avoid being hit on the shins. I wonder if we have to put them back?

Itchy… itchy… ITCHY

Chiquita and I have been suffering from hay fever (that's what the Woman calls it). It makes us sneeze many times and we are very itchy and scratching a lot. The Woman gave us both a nice refreshing bath with a special shampoo that felt really good.

After the bath we were allowed to air dry. We can only do this by having zoomies up and down the stairs and out into the garden at breakneck speed. Chiquita told the Woman that she hates the noise of the hairdryer and that it ruffles our fur and makes us feel uncomfortable. She said, "Okay, then, you dry yourselves."

There was not a soul around downstairs when I spotted a plate full of sandwiches sitting on the table. It looked so lonely and inviting that I climbed on the chair and started tucking in. Immediately, the Woman yelled from upstairs "SHAGGY! Get off the table now!" How did she know that I was eating the sandwiches? Does she have eyes in the back of her head? It's no good telling me off. You left your sandwiches on the table and walked away. I saved them from falling on the floor or getting curled up and dry. Huh! You can't please some people, can you?

Listen up humans!
This is what our tail wags mean

We met many dogs from different countries this morning and I stopped and chatted to each one. I learned to say hello in Polish, German and Lithuanian; of course, I already knew it in French, Italian, Spanish and English. Greybeard said he was very impressed at how fluent I had become in foreign languages. I am probably best at Doglish. I am going to teach Greybeard and the Woman about the meanings of Tail Wags.

1. When I hold my tail straight up pointing to the sky, it means I am alert and excited.
2. If my tail is straight out, it shows other dogs that I am neutral and exploring.

3. If my tail is down, then you can be sure I am nervous and concerned about something or someone.
4. If my tail is half down (or half mast, as Greybeard calls it) and not wagging, it means that I am very nervous.
5. If I wag my tail very fast and furiously in round circles, it means that I am super excited about something or to see you.
6. Gentle broad strokes mean I am happy and contented.
7. Wagging to the right is to show that someone I have just met is a good person.
8. Low tail moving at the tip says I am unsure about a situation.
9. I am anxious if I am using short up and down strokes.
10. Loud thumping tail proves that life is good and I am pleased.
11. Tail straight between my legs says "Oh! My god! I am really scared."

A woman threw a ball for her mutt this morning. I joined in the chase, but the woman started yelling "Don't take his ball!" I stopped chasing and went back to the Woman and told her, "I didn't want his dirty, stinking, germ-laden, manky ball. So there!" The mutt looked at me apologetically and said, "Sorry! She is a very neurotic person and gets very personal about me and the ball."

Woof down, or as the humans call it, "lock down"

The humans are going through something called Lockdown and there are big signs everywhere in parks saying "Dogs must be on a Lead", and Woman bought a double lead so that Chiquita and I are tied together. Then she added it to a 15-metre-long lead. When we get to the park, she drops the lead and lets us run anywhere that we want. When a busybody comes along and says, "Your dogs should be on a lead," she answers, "They are on a lead." Clever or what? And it's such fun when we go either side of them.

Both Chiquita and I were overjoyed to meet up with one of our best and nicest friends – little Oscar, the Shih Tzu. He is a delightful little chap and we always have great fun when he comes to stay. If you shout at him, he never takes it personally and he is so good-natured. He is always up for a game of tag. Chiquita adores him. He tells us, "I love my mum and dad and sisters, but I always want to come home with you because I have such a good time at your house.

"Are you still chasing that stupid squirrel? Do you remember the time that I nearly caught him when he fell off the fence in panic?"

Greybeard and the Woman think that they are being so clever when they talk to each other and say, "Shall we take them for a 'Double-You-A-Ell-Kay'?" Honestly, they really believe that we are stupid, but they don't realize that the word "shall" is what we associate with walks. It's all right; we won't tell them. They can go through life thinking it's the word "walk" that will get us going.

The toy box

I've just found the box that is crammed with stinky toys, balls, frisbees and other marvellous things. Pulling them all out and scattering them everywhere was such marvellous fun. I will take the toy lamb and pull out all the white stuffing. Can't eat the stuff but it is very therapeutic pulling it out and leaving it all over the floor.

Oh! I've just found a pen thing that the Woman writes with. It doesn't taste of anything but it is crunchy and it is cleaning my teeth.

Chiquita and I have decided that we have got used to the vacuum cleaner. It's an evil contraption. We don't trust it all. It growls and snarls and its sole purpose is to get clogged up with hair and then Greybeard gets angry and has to clean it out. "It's bloody dog hair," he yells. We hide because we don't know if we have done something wrong.

A man in the park stopped to pet Chiquita and me this morning, and said that we were such pretty dogs and so good too. The Woman said, "Sometimes," so I glared at her. I hope she picked up the message that she shouldn't stop strangers from saying nice things about us. Just for that I will refuse to go to her when she wants to pet me. Woman can't say nasty things and then expect to be cuddled.

Met Lizzie, the Pit Bull cross who used to be a bait dog for fighting. She said it was very terrifying, as they would use her so that other dogs could get into the mood for fighting. She told us that the warrior dogs would bite her really hard and it was a competition to see who bites the hardest before they set on each other. Then a lovely kind man adopted her and now her life is full of love, kindness and being spoilt. She says her owner gets very concerned for her and tells everyone that she is very nervous, but she told us, "That's okay. It gives him something to fret about and I love him dearly. I love it especially when I can hang my head out of the car window or when my dad puts the top down and I can feel the breeze in my fur."

Have you noticed how a human will yawn if we have a big yawn. I often play tricks on them by sitting facing them, then giving a big yawn. They start yawning and saying things like, "I'm not tired, just relaxed. Why are you yawning, dog? You're not tired, are you? It's all that dashing up and down the playing fields that makes you sleep until 4.30 p.m., isn't it?"

I don't know what made me do it, but I managed to get the rubbish bin lid open and pull out an empty yo-ghurt pot. I was really deep into licking it clean when I heard the Woman yell, "What have you got there? You rubbish hound." So I ran into the garden with it in my mouth and continued to lick it clean. I can't explain why I did it – there really was no reason. Sometimes we dogs have this compulsion to eat garbage. It must be something that is in my genes.

Luna, the beagle that lives across the road, smiled and waved at me as we were getting ready to get into the car for our afternoon walk. She always sits at the window and watches the world go by. She looks like a friendly little thing, so I may just invite her over to have a play day with us. She goes for a walk in a place called Hampstead Heath. I will have to ask Greybeard if it will be okay to invite her over to our house.

Uh, oh! The doorbell just went and woke Chiquita and me from a deep sleep. We rushed to the front door, barking furiously. Then we heard Greybeard yelling, "It's on the TV, dimbos. It's on the TV, so quieten down." Sometimes you feel such an idiot when something like that happens. Well! We weren't to know. It sounded as real as can be.

T-shirts, coats and other unmentionables

It's raining! It's pouring. Oh god, no. Please don't put those see-through plastic coats on us. They make a crinkly sound and those shoulder pad things make us walk sideways, like crabs. All the other dogs in the park sneer and titter at us because they say we are wearing cling-film coats. The big butch guys always mutter insults at us. Mind you, we don't look as bad as some of those dogs in full-on pyjamas. Why do the owners choose such bright colours? Now, those are the dogs I really feel sorry for.

Ooooops! I think I had better keep a low profile. I've just heard Greybeard asking, "Where have the biscuits I left on the table gone to? Did you finish them?" Kept quiet, but they had looked and smelled so inviting that I thought I would nibble one... and then thought "what the hell" and took the lot. And delicious they were too. Sorry, Chiquita, you missed out because you were snoozing.

Eric the Wawa (Chihuaha) was yelling over the fence that he has been feeling a bit depressed lately. I asked him what there was to be depressed about. I told him, "You have a five-star life style: more food than you can eat, smothered in love and attention, sleeping in your human's bed, lots of toys, and me and Chiquita as friends. What's brought all this on?" He said, "Dunno. I get like this sometimes. There must be more to life than just barking and reading pee-mails on trees and lamp posts."

Group sun bathing

It's a beautiful day. Hot and sunny. The best place to stretch out and catch the rays is right outside the bathroom door. Sunbathing is paradise. It gets the fur warm, the skin feels glowing, and scratching makes all the nerve ends tingle. When we have two or three other dogs to say, we all stretch out together.

The woman says that as Chiquita and I are white, we would need sun cream on our noses to stop us getting sunburnt if we went to a beach.

Little Bertie, the Norfolk, or is it Norwich, Terrier – never know which – came to stay. He followed me everywhere. He is still very young and I told him to do what I do so that he learns properly. I showed him how to go downstairs without knocking down the barrier, to pee where I pee and to sniff the best smells.

His mum said he is deeply traumatised by going in the car, but when I said, "Get in," he jumped in right away. We told him he was a con artist for putting his mum through the worry. He grinned and said, "It's the best way to get to sit on her lap in the front seat."

Oh, dear! I was busy gnawing on a big tripe bone and because I couldn't get my mouth around it properly, I picked it up and moved to my bed to get comfortable and eat it there. As I picked it up, the Woman walked by in her bare feet. The bone dropped out of my mouth onto her foot. She hopped up and down yelling, "Ow! Ow! Ow! That really hurt, Shags. Was it really necessary?" I put on my best soulful look, wagged my tail and licked her foot to say sorry. I hope she realizes that I didn't do it on purpose.

Trying to be friendly

On my walk last night I thought I would be friendly, so I smiled and wagged my tail at a lady with a long black frock and a cover over her face. She screamed and backed away as though I was about to attack her. My Woman said, "It's okay, Shags, I know you were being friendly but not all Middle Eastern people like dogs. It's their religion. They believe that dogs are unclean. We all know that you are especially when you roll in disgusting things." Okay, okay. You don't have to keep on about it. I am trying very hard to control my urges but when they come on, my mind goes blank and it just happens.

Drat! A mini sausage has just rolled under the kitchen cabinet and my paw isn't long enough to reach it. "Go on, Chiquita, put on your most appealing look and the Woman will get it out for you. Get ready! Here she comes now! Well done! I think she will give us a sausage each as she believes in being fair." What did you just hide in that mini sausage? It looked like a pill.

Why have you just got down the suitcase? Are you going somewhere? Are we coming with you? You know how insecure a suitcase makes me. If you put it on the floor and open it, you know that I will get in and lie in it.

Chiquita and I are well travelled, as our other mum used to take us everywhere, so we know what a suit-case means.

Meeting celebs

Today we met a famous man with his two dogs. He patted me on the head, but his smaller dog, who was on a lead and came from Romania, didn't like that.

She lunged at me and said, "Gerroff! He's my dad, so stop trying to suck up to him."

I said, "Chill! No one wants to take your dad away from you. I already have the nice Greybeard, so there!"

It was such hot weather today that the Woman said, "You poor little dogs! You both look so hot." She put something called a fan on the floor and switched it on. It was blowing cool air and it felt really good as we lay in front of it and let the breeze gently ruffle our fur. This is the life, I thought.

Chiquita and I really love our walks

I know you think that I am crazy, but I do lose my mind with joy when I hear the words "Lets go!" There is no other option. Every day people smile at us, talk to us, reach down to pat us and ruffle our fur and completely ignore the Woman. Best of all they slip us little treats. We now know the people who carry treats and will find them somewhere in the park and get our treats. Woman says, "I'm not surprised that the vet thinks you have put on weight. You both resemble puffer fish dressed in white fur."

I really hate it when you treat me like an idiot.

Okay, I agree with you. I have acted like an idiot in the past and tried to spit it out, but it's only because you force open my mouth and stick the pill right down my throat. It makes me want to throw up.

Not a good day today

First, I get yelled at for eating rubbish in the park.

Then I get yelled at for rolling in fox shit and I know I will be getting a shower. Then I get yelled at for digging up the flowerbed. Then I get yelled at for barking too long at the bottom of the garden. Now I am wet from the shower and lying in my basket. Oy vey! What a day I have had! Sigh!

Now I am wet from the shower and lying in my basket.

Losing my mind

The excitement of being in the park just got to me this morning and I completely forgot where I was and went out of a gate and onto the road. I was very confident and walked down the middle of the road with many cars and bicyclists whizzing around. A stranger rushed out of the park and stood in the middle of the road to get me back into the park.

The Woman was very angry with me and said, "Idiot! You could have been killed. Don't ever do that again." She immediately put on my lead and led me back to the car. I could sense she was very angry with me because she would not speak to me, touch me or smile for two whole days no matter how much grovelling I did. Oh, dear! I think I have been very stupid. Chiquita agrees with me.

Ice-cream! Yum! Yum!

Coming home from the park last week, the Woman suddenly said, "I fancy an ice-cream".

We stopped by the ice-cream van and she bought two cones with chocolate sticking out of them and came back to the car. She put some on her fingers for Chiquita and me to lick off. She asked, "Have you ever had ice-cream, Shags? It numbs your tongue and you will go 'Mnnuff' instead of bark." It was really cold, tasted sweet and made my lips curl up. It was delicious and she left a little in each cone end. Yes! I could go for ice-cream in a big way. Definitely! Bring it on!

Have you ever had your teeth brushed? The Woman put a rubber thing on her finger with some toothpaste on it, opened my mouth and brushed all the way around. It tasted good and minty, so I didn't struggle. She brushed my teeth because I had munched on something crispy and tasty that Greybeard said smelled gross. They both called me a disgusting, gross animal with disgusting habits. I hate it when they get angry with me.

Vet bills cost more than gravy bones

Met a giant Great Dane in the park today. Named Freddy, he was so huge that I couldn't reach his balls to sniff them.

He was a really nice gentle lad and said he felt lonely because when people saw him, they moved away in fear and wouldn't let their dogs come near him. I think I will make friends with him, because he seemed so nice and kind. Looking like a giant, he will always be a safe dog to be with.

It was so windy in the park this morning that all of the dogs that we met were complaining that it made us look like that actor Butternut Cumberfloof, with our fur being blown in all directions. Little Chiquita was being blown off her paws and having great difficulty staying upright. I had to be careful not to pee against that wind, otherwise it would go into my face.

Met a lovely lumbering Labrador named Leo, who told us that he is obsessed with tennis balls. He says his party trick is to see how many balls he can stuff into his mouth. His goal is 10 at once. "Don't ask me why? Maybe it goes back to puppyhood, when people would take them away from me to stop me ripping them apart."

Girls who roll over for me

Chiquita went to the vet today because she got a grass seed in her paw two weeks ago and it wasn't healing. They gave her pills and a crown of shame, as the lady called it. This was to stop her constantly licking her paw. Clever little thing! She discovered that if she stretched her paw out, she could reach it without banging her head against the cone around her neck. Greybeard looked at the bill and said, "Phew! It would have been better if I had sent you both to an expensive dog kennels for one week, as it cost just as much."

Today was a bad day for me too, as I have not been forgiven for being disobedient in the park a week ago and begging for food from many different picnickers. I got temporary amnesia and did it again. Only this time I refused to come back when called. A stranger started chasing me so that the Woman could catch me. She was furious when she put me on the lead and dragged me back to the car. She slapped me and said, "You will listen when I call you. You bad, disobedient dog." I could tell that she was really, really angry because she wouldn't stroke or cuddle me and she looked angry all evening. I am definitely going to be as good as gold tomorrow.

A man had his dog, Indigo, on a tight lead and told us that he never lets him off the lead, because he attacks other dogs. We sniffed each other and wagged tails and he told me, "Chill and don't be afraid – I won't really do anything, but if I see other dogs, I might lunge at them and give their owners a heart attack." We both laughed, "Heh, heh, heh! That's really Wicked!" A dog needs excitement occasionally.

I am a sucker for a pretty girl. I have fallen in love with an adorable little Cavachon named Smudge. She really is a gorgeous little thing, who doesn't seem full of herself. When I see her in the park, we romp together and it is bliss, for I am just a boy, standing in front of a pretty girl, asking her to roll in fox poo with me. And she does, without question. We often dream of meeting incognito in a new park, where I can say to strangers, "Yes! I'll have that treat and be sure to throw one to that little bitch standing nearby!"

Of course I believe in the power of barking. One of the reasons that I am alive today is because of the barking. Everyday a postman approaches my home and everyday I bark until I hear the gate bang shut and him leave. To this day he still has not brutally murdered Greybeard, the Woman or Chiquita. And I can safely say I have the power of barking to thank for that.

My philosophy about foraging among trash that it is better to have eaten something and thrown it up, then eaten it again than never having eaten it at all. What's disgusting about that? I know of many dogs who really enjoy doing that. It's known as doggie bulimia.

Chill out caninos!

Every dog that we met this morning was in a grumpy mood. A black Poodle named Felix warned us not to come near, as he was really irritated about being stripped at the groomers and made to look like a Whippet. "It's very cooling not to have so much fur, but I hate the stupid pompon they have given me on my tail. It looks like the Flag of Surrender."

Then we met an aggressive young Bitzer, who suddenly attacked Chiquita for no good reason. He thought she was in a fighting mood.

"Chill!" I said, "My sister is the most docile, friendliest little girl ever. Why don't you have a word with your owner and ask her to stop feeding you such high-protein food. It's turning you into a Hound of the Baskerville."

"I know! I know!" he said, "but this heat makes me irritable and itchy. Apologies!"

Happiness

Chiquita is feeling happy today. Her foot must be less painful. She threw herself on her back on the grass and wriggled around with the biggest smile on her face, kicking her legs in the air. She was singing at the top of her voice:

> *"I'M H.A.P.P.Y!*
> *I'M H.A.P.P.Y!*
> *I know I am.*
> *I'm sure I am.*
> *I'M H.A.P.P.Y!"*

It's so good seeing her so happy.

She challenged me to a race and we belted around the playing field chasing each other. Something that looks like the Monster from the Deep is rushing towards us. Good God! It's that Shih Tzu named Pumpkin. His soul purpose for living is to search out puddles in the park and to wade through them so that he is covered in wet mud. "You have no idea how empowering it is to have a good swim every morning. It drives my owner crazy, but since we don't live too far, she doesn't mind the rude remarks and looks of pity that she gets from other dog owners on our way home. She is very kind and always gives me a shower when we get home." We don't get to see Pumpkin much, as he walks at a different time to us, but he regularly leaves us pee-mails of his life. I remember when he stayed with us for one week, he loved eating fruit and vegetables. We've picked up his habit now and the Woman gives us different fruits for breakfast. Our favourite is watermelon or "Watta mey-lone", as Jimmy the Dachshund calls it. He pronounces it the French way.

We have a new guest staying for a few days. Lily the Lurcher arrived looking very nervous but once her owner had gone, she loosened up and joined us in squirrel hunting in the garden. Chiquita whispered, "She is so elegant, I hate her already." She was only joking. Lily was really nice and told us that her dad owns restaurants and sometimes brings home a treat for her. On the first morning after she arrived, she put her paws on our neighbour's wall, then said to us, "I'm going to jump over there over and have a quick pee." She did this at every opportunity. When we were all sitting around chatting, she mentioned that her uncle was a Prime Minister or something and she would sometimes stay in his house, which had big gardens and a wood to walk in that was full of rabbits and other animals. We liked having her to stay and maybe one day she will come back and visit us. It was enjoyable walking alongside someone who was tall and elegant. Every dog in the park wanted to know us.

While we were waiting at traffic lights, I shouted out of the car window to Paco and Elvis, the two very well-dressed pocket-sized Chihuahuas. "Eh, gringos! What you bin up to? Haven't seen you for months." Paco said, "Same old, same old! What about you?" Every day they have on a different outfit. Lovely lads who travel to Greece a lot and tell us that it's good fun swimming in the hot sea. I couldn't catch up with their news, as Greybeard was in a hurry and we raced off in the car. Every day they have on a different outfit.

The sadness of some dogs

A little Bitzer named Fizz was sadly walking past us this morning and tried to exchange sniffs, but her owner yanked her away roughly. I asked her if this was her daily routine and she said, "Yes. I am at home all day when they go out to work and the only excitement I get is when delivery men or the postman comes to the door and calls out my name and say hello." She added sadly, "I hope that one day someone will tell my owners that meeting other dogs, bottom sniffing and reading pees are very important to keep a dog happy."

I asked Greybeard why people bother to get dogs and then keep them locked up like prisoners. I did feel so sorry for Fizz and said that we would look out for her in the park and rush over and talk to her. She looked pleased about that. Chiquita and I are very lucky to have found our forever people.

What a wonderful walk this afternoon. We met the two Chinese Bichons. They speak fluent Chinese, but, for us, trying to bark in that language is impossible, especially if you get it wrong. I don't want to be yelling "Chopsticks! Chopsticks!" and find that I am yelling something rude. We bumped into little Oscar, the Shih Tzu. Our people were trying to avoid seeing each other, as they know how excited we get at, but then Oscar spotted us. It was a very ecstatic meeting and passers-by stopped to stare and smile at our excitement. Oscar's owner said, "Oh, god! I'll never get him home, so I'll keep him on the lead or he will join you on your walk."

Stanley, the all-black Yorkiepoo, who has joined the Black Lives Matter movement to show his solidarity for all things black, told us that he can't stop as he has many balls to chase.

Later we were joined by Caspar, the yodelling Schnauzer who is always practising his art. His ambition is to win *Britain's Got Talent* as the UK's first yodelling Schnauzer. He wants to be known as The Great Casparelli.

Neighbourhood moggies

A new cat has moved in two doors away. He acts as though he owns the entire street. He was in our garden and when I rushed out, he took on the full battle mode, arching his back and snarling at me. I said to him, "Listen, motherpupper, don't get hissy with me. You are on my property. You are trespassing. You're the new kid on the block, so respect is what you need to show to residents who have been here a long time." Of course he doesn't know that I've only lived here for one year, but if you don't set the ground rules now, before long he will be yowling with his mates in my garden at 4 a.m. I told him that the last thing he would enjoy is a bucket of cold water thrown out of the bedroom window. He skulked off glaring at me and muttering under his fur. "And you," I said.

Dog rules

Do you think that its too presumptious of me to give Greybeard and Woman a list of my rules?
- Don't come home stinking of other dogs.
- You must feed me a bit of every goodie that you eat.
- Don't coochy-coo me, then trick me into the bath.
- It's good to let me out even if I have only just come in. There was a spot I forgot to smell.

- Don't shush me when you are talking on the phone. I could have sworn I heard the doorbell ring.
- Don't move me when I am asleep in the middle of the bed. You have more than enough room on the edge of your side.
- If something falls on the floor, its mine.
- Don't expect to go to the toilet on your own.

The return of the tree rat

Grrrr! It's that damned tree rat again. This time he was being humble and friendly. He was sitting quietly on the fence with his paws clasped and he says, "Excuse me, do you think they will be filling up the bird feeder soon? The others wanted me to ask." Damned nerve! He digs up all the newly planted bulbs and plants, and tries to plant his peanuts in all the flowerpots. I am not squirrelist, but he does take liberties with the Woman's kindness. Scoot off and go find peanuts from some other soft resident. Hmmm!

Zoom meeting with the vet

Greybeard told us to sit quietly and watch the screen because the vet wanted to have a Zoom video conference call with us. Chiquita and I had no idea what it was about, but we did as we were told. The vet came on screen and startling droning on about the data he was given and our records. When he started speaking, I had this urge to lick my balls. Licking my balls seems to be a rite of passage among my clan. He got upset and asked me to "switch off the screen" if I wanted to do such things in public.

He said that the records showed that 340 were terrorized by us but none were caught. That was really good, he said. Chiquita fell asleep and the vet said, "Unbelievable! Low attention span. Pay attention, miss, will you!" She got out a squeaky toy and started making a noise. The vet got very irritable and said, "There is no point in continuing this meeting," and switched off.

I always pee on Greybeard and the Woman when they come home because I am so happy to see them. None of my doggy friends pee when they see me, which makes me think that I am surrounded by fake furry friends.

Leo, our most favourite person in the world, stopped by to say hello this afternoon. He speaks Spanish and always chats to us in our language. Chiquita started flirting and looking wide-eyed and pretty. He gives us both equal amounts of cuddles. I wonder if I should save a gravy bone for him as a thank you for being so nice.

Well, that's the story of my life so far. I am sure there are plenty of exciting times ahead, and I'll be recording them for another book.

Why not join me in some bottom sniffing and until the next time?